Heavy Words
Lightly Thrown

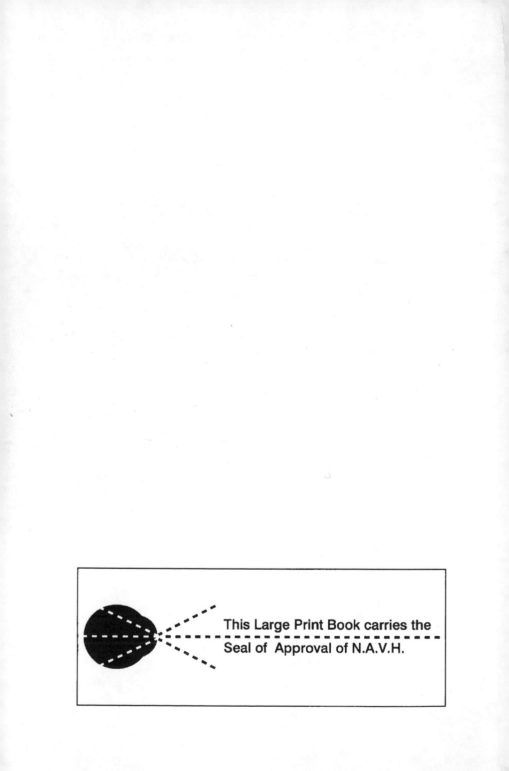

This Large Print Book carries the
Seal of Approval of N.A.V.H.

Heavy Words Lightly Thrown

The Reason Behind The Rhyme

Chris Roberts

Thorndike Press • Waterville, Maine

Published in 2006 by arrangement with Gotham Books,
a division of Penguin Group (USA) Inc.

Thorndike Press® Large Print Nonfiction.

The tree indicium is a trademark of Thorndike Press.

The text of this Large Print edition is unabridged.
Other aspects of the book may vary from the original edition.

Set in 16 pt. Plantin by Elena Picard.

Printed in the United States on permanent paper.

Library of Congress Cataloging-in-Publication Data

Roberts, Chris.
    Heavy words lightly thrown : the reason behind the rhyme
/ by Chris Roberts.
      p. cm. — (Thorndike Press large print nonfiction)
    ISBN 0-7862-8517-6 (lg. print : hc : alk. paper)
    1. Nursery rhymes, English — History and criticism.
2. Large type books. I. Title. II. Thorndike Press large
print nonfiction series.
    PR976.R55 2006
    398.8′0942—dc22   2006001519

Heavy Words Lightly Thrown

As the Founder/CEO of NAVH, the only national health agency solely devoted to those who, although not totally blind, have an eye disease which could lead to serious visual impairment, I am pleased to recognize Thorndike Press* as one of the leading publishers in the large print field.

Founded in 1954 in San Francisco to prepare large print textbooks for partially seeing children, NAVH became the pioneer and standard setting agency in the preparation of large type.

Today, those publishers who meet our standards carry the prestigious "Seal of Approval" indicating high quality large print. We are delighted that Thorndike Press is one of the publishers whose titles meet these standards. We are also pleased to recognize the significant contribution Thorndike Press is making in this important and growing field.

Lorraine H. Marchi, L.H.D.
Founder/CEO
NAVH

* Thorndike Press encompasses the following imprints: Thorndike, Wheeler, Walker and Large Print Press.

Contents

Preface to the US Edition

I've often taken small groups of Americans on walking tours around London. If someone doesn't understand something I've said, it's easy to fix: I simply glance up and register the raised eyebrow or hand gesture (international sign language for "What is this guy on about?"), and correct my spiel accordingly. With a book, that's a shade trickier, and I was concerned. Because whilst the theme of nursery rhymes is shared by our cultures, indeed most of them were around when we were one nation under a groove together, my cultural references are very British.

However, the good people at Gotham came up with a solution: a glossary for the US edition. I would like to think that writing this explanatory vocabulary list was a good deal of fun because it enabled me to reconsider just "What is this guy on about?" In fact, I'm not sure if it shouldn't have been included in the revised UK edition as well, because many of my learned British readers have also missed some of the references in the text. So this isn't just the usual case of two countries divided by a common language. I appear to be quite an island within an island, St. Helena'd in my own country, as well.

The glossary and this fresh preface aside, this is the same revised and expanded text that Granta published in the UK in October 2004. They helped to tidy up the original text, provided space for more rhymes that economic considerations had kept out of the first edition, and generally made it a more rounded and satisfying product.

The very first version of *Heavy Words Lightly Thrown* was published in November 2003 with a print run of two thousand (and I'd like to thank here and now the intrepid eighty-seven Americans who braved the vagaries of my Web site to order it). There was no thought of a glossary in that edition, there was not even, as I suggest above, enough capital to put all of the rhymes in, and as for the idea that I would have to reconsider the contents with a worldwide audience in mind, the thought never occurred to me. After modest sales over the Christmas 2003 period, the book suddenly and surprisingly went global. This, at a point when there was not even a decent UK distribution network set up. Now is perhaps not the time or place to dwell on some of the more surreal events of early March 2004, but suffice to say that I never expected to be called a "boffin"* by a South African newspaper, or to have the dubious distinction of being (as far as I am aware) the only person to have said "gonorrhea" on a certain daytime talk show.

F and M Publications (responsible for the first edition) was a company I set up with the support of a group of friends. The idea was to provide a forum through which various barking schemes and beautiful projects could be brought into being with the vague notion that each project would fund the next and the company would grow organically in that way. *Heavy Words* was the first such project. Quite simply, no one involved was able to cope with the demands that the unexpected publicity brought our way and, on a more personal level, it was July 2004 before my living room ceased to resemble a dispatch

*Terms that may be unfamiliar to American readers are indicated by an asterisk, and can be found in the glossary on page 240.

13

office run by gibbons.

So it should be clear that the first edition of *Heavy Words Lightly Thrown* was a very Mickey Rooney, "Let's put the show on here, kids" project. Favours were called in, offices temporarily squatted*, materials and money borrowed, corners cut, and an awful lot of people put in an awful lot of work without pay (though this has since been sorted out).

The revised edition contains all the rhymes intended for the first, and more, including *Yankee Doodle* and *Rock a Bye Baby*, both of which have clear American associations. *Yankee Doodle* is particularly interesting in that its use by the US forces after the War of Independence showed a gift for comic timing and irony that some on this side of the Atlantic claim Americans lack. You'd think after *The Simpsons*, *South Park*, *Frasier*, and countless other top-notch comedy shows, they'd have been disabused of that notion, but there's no accounting for some folk.

So I'm confident that the book will make you laugh, in places at least, inform you about some odder aspects of, mostly, British history, and provide you with some nice stories to relate as well as some interesting new vocabulary to play about with.

I'm delighted to have this opportunity to speak to a wider American audience than I'm accustomed to — and I apologize in advance for any residual misunderstanding.

Introduction

It should come as no surprise that nursery rhymes are full of sex, death, and cruelty. After all, children can be very vicious themselves. Over the centuries, though, traditional meanings have been lost and harsher versions of some rhymes subtly neutered, while others have fallen victim to changing cultural assumptions. All of these factors have caused the original point of many of the rhymes to be lost. This book attempts to rewrite the rewrites and rediscover lost meanings. At the very least, it presents some theories about what those lost meanings might be.

How adult songs such as "Oranges and Lemons" and "Goosie, Goosie Gander" — often highly sexual, often politically satirical — came to be rhymes read to children is almost a book in itself. Some were clearly adult rhymes that were sung to children because they were the only rhymes an adult knew. Others were deliberately created as a simple way to tell children a story or give them information: for example, "London's Burning" ("There once was a great fire in London"). Some were clearly partisan, almost gloating, in the manner of football chants*, while others conveyed more complex ideas in code, in order to avoid appearing disloyal to a monarch, for example. Like rhyming slang*, many rhymes would have deliberately sought to hide their meaning from the uninitiated. Monarchists, for example, might have been cautious about singing "Little Boy Blue" in front of Cromwell's men. In the same way that we have satire and irony on television today, songs and rhymes were clearly much more popular routes in the past.

What makes the search for meaning harder is that many nursery rhymes are just nonsense verse made up of pleasing sounds. Sometimes it's impossible to know which have a story behind them and which do not. For example:

Higgledy Piggledy my black hen,
She lays eggs for gentlemen.
Gentlemen come every day,
To see what my black hen has laid.

This could be about a hen. It could be, as some believe, about prostitution. It could even be about a specific prostitute or be based on an earlier, more direct, rhyme:

Little Blue Betty lived in a den,
She sold good ale to gentlemen.
Gentlemen came every day,
And little Blue Betty hopped away.
She hopped upstairs to make her bed,
And she tumbled down and broke her
  head.

Further speculation includes the suggestion that the "black hen" represents a spy feeding someone information, with the word "black" meaning dark or evil, the "eggs" representing gossip or rumour, and "hen" being used as a derogatory name for a male. Then again, it could be about a female spy. Or it could be about a gay spy (something Britain excels at). Then again, maybe it's about a beautiful black woman, or just a woman with black hair and the many suitors whom she keeps at arm's length by telling them stories, as did Odysseus's wife.

In all probability, the rhyme is just about a hen that is a good layer. Similarly, it's highly likely that once somebody's son called John did go to bed with his trousers on and his mother elected to commemorate the event with the rhyme "Diddle, Diddle Dumpling, My Son John." The difficulty is, once you start seeing meaning you can find it anywhere, and people have been looking a long time. As with conspiracy theories today, if you start with the assumption that there is an ulterior meaning, it is much easier to find one. So this collection attempts to strain out the more outlandish theories and select those for which there is most historical support.

Because the sense and associations of rhymes shifted over the centuries, even before their current incarnation as innocent verse for children, some of the rhymes' initial meanings came to be superseded by events at a particular time. This is certainly true of "Grand Old Duke of York," which was based on an earlier rhyme, "Brave Old King of France," but was changed to refer to Frederick, Duke of York. It was also very likely the case with "Humpty-Dumpty," an old rhyme that became associated with a cannon during the English Civil War. And even in our own time, if you ask people for an association with the song "You'll Never Walk Alone," many people will say Liverpool Football Club rather than the perfectly innocent Rodgers and Hammerstein musical *Carousel* that the Koppites* plundered it from.

The move towards sanitizing rhymes for

children accelerated in the Victorian era, with its radically altered view of childhood, its recognition of childhood as a concept. Prior to that, little thought was given to shielding "adult sights" from children, even if it had been possible to do so. During the nineteenth century the rhymes were increasingly written up, illustrated, and sold as collections for children. This took them off the streets and into the parlours, making them at once more accessible but perhaps less potent. It would not do to blame the Victorians entirely for the loss of meaning in nursery rhymes, as it's quite probable that some had already lost their point before then, and many were certainly written down prior to the nineteenth century. The Victorians were keen on deliberately rewriting them, however, as opposed to accidentally mistranslating them, in a bid to tidy the rhymes and give moral instruction. For the first time in British history, there was the beginning of a division between adult and children's entertainment. Prior to that, children would be swigging ale and smoking ciggies down the bear pit like everyone else. It is perhaps odd that some of these "adult rhymes" ended up on the children's side of the fence, although the process might have been assisted by the huge population shifts from the countryside to cities, which served to break up local oral traditions and take the rhymes out of their original context.

The constitutional reforms and political struggles of the nineteenth century reduced the necessity for clever allegorical topical songs, and protest no longer had to be conducted quite so covertly. There was no need for a complex, sly rhyme when you could stand up and call the queen a humourless, plum-faced parasite out loud and direct (well, at least in theory). Increasing literacy and improved communications added to a new, more up-front political style in Britain, which was underlined by the revolutions of 1848 throughout Europe. Catholic enemies (whether internal or external) ceased to be of concern. Britain (no Scotland to worry about now, after the Act of Union*) was comfortably Protestant and, while it might be overstating the case to say that there was no sectarianism left, Catholics were certainly no longer being executed by the state for their beliefs. The same was true of continental Europe. For one hundred years after Napoleon, Britain virtually ceased to see Europe as a serious concern, preferring to look out to the world beyond the Continent. Remember, this is a small island off Europe that could come up with the newspaper headline "Fog in Channel. Continent Cut Off."

It would be untrue, however, to say that the British today have entirely lost their talent for subversive song. The title of this book is lifted from a band, the Smiths, who are a good example of a British pop culture that has been a world leader for much of the last forty years, certainly in tackling difficult subjects through song. Furthermore, the desire for communal tribal chanting has not left even the most sanitized of football stadia. The songs may be less subtle in that context but, three hundred years from now, historians might well puzzle over this tirade of abuse myself and thousands of others had to suffer at Goodison Park* in the twenty-first century:

> You are a Scouser*, an ugly Scouser,
> You're only happy on giro* day.
> Your mum's out thieving,
> Your dad's drug dealing,
> Please don't take our hubcaps away.

Who knows, one day this might end up

23

as a lullaby, with future etymologists pondering what a "hubcap" was and what "giro" could mean. In any case, it's certainly no more vicious than a number of the rhymes collected here.

Although some of these rhymes appear to have their origins in the Middle Ages, the golden age for nursery rhymes lies in the years between the Tudors and the end of the Stuarts. This was Britain's formative period, covering roughly a quarter of a millennium and bringing with it the Act of Union, the Industrial Revolution, the Reformation, the Civil War, the growth of Empire and trading, the Glorious Revolution, William Shakespeare, the King James Bible, Isaac Newton, and much, much else besides. These were heady topics, even for the world's largest language to cope with. So why not keep it short and tell it in rhyme? Teach the children to glory in tales with hidden depths: in heavy words lightly thrown.

Little Jack Horner

Little Jack Horner
Sat in the corner
Eating his Christmas pie.
He stuck in his thumb,
Pulled out a plum
And said "What a good boy am I!"

Little "Jack" Horner was actually Thomas Horner, steward to the Abbot of Glastonbury during the reign of King Henry VIII. Shortly after the dissolution of the monasteries, Mr. Horner settled into a very comfortable house. The rhyme tells the story of his acquisition of the property.

Always keen to raise fresh funds, Henry had shown an interest in Glastonbury (and other abbeys). Hoping to appease the royal appetite, the nervous Abbot, Richard Whiting, allegedly sent Thomas Horner to the King with a special gift. This was a pie containing the title deeds to twelve manor houses in the hope that these would deflect the King from acquiring Glastonbury

25

Abbey. On his way to London, the not so loyal courier Horner apparently stuck his thumb into the pie and extracted the deeds for Mells Manor, a plum piece of real estate. The attempted bribe failed and the dissolution of the monasteries (including Glastonbury) went ahead from 1536 to 1540. Richard Whiting was subsequently executed, but the Horner family kept the house, so the moral of this one is: treachery and greed pay off, but bribery is a bad idea.

The only problem with this fantastic story is that the Horner family deny any wrongdoing on the part of their ancestor and claim that the property was bought fair and square at the time, along with various others. Then again, they would say that, wouldn't they? A great deal of property did change hands rather cheaply during the dissolution, however, so maybe Jack (né Thomas) was just legally taking a decent slice of the pie on offer rather than illegally stealing it. There can be no doubt that the land was stolen from the Church, but perhaps it might be fairer to see it as some sort of redistribution by the state whereby land was taken from corrupt landlords and given to productive members of society. That is certainly one of the ways in which Henry VIII and his ministers presented it at the time.

Henry was a cunning politician and was surrounded by able and ambitious ministers, well able to exploit a situation for both personal gain and political effect. In 1531, laws were passed to limit the gathering of papal revenue in England. This was a response to Pope Clement VII's refusal to annul Henry's marriage to Catherine of Aragon. To be fair to the papacy, they had granted a special licence to allow the marriage in the first place, as Catherine was the widow of Henry's brother. The divorce went through in 1533 and, in 1534, the Act of Supremacy was passed, making the monarch the head of the Church in England. This might have all looked rather sordid if in 1535 the Vicar-General of the Church in England, Thomas Cromwell, had not started a large-scale investigation into conduct within the Catholic Church and in particular within the monasteries. Corrupt clergy have been a staple of English comedy since the language was first written down and very probably before. *Piers Plowman* and *The Canterbury Tales* both contain outright attacks on the Church, and movements for reform flourished across Europe and in England throughout the Middle Ages. In 1517, Martin Luther nailed his complaints to a church door and by 1525 was conducting mass in German. Cromwell used his investigation and Luther's theological arguments to deflect attention away from the activities of the King and towards the behaviour of the Church.

The Catholic Church drew half its annual income from its ownership of around one-quarter of the cultivated land in England and Wales. The confiscation of this land would not only provide Henry with a great deal of cash but also deprive his enemies of it. At first, in 1536, nearly four hundred of the smaller monasteries were closed and their land sold to local merchants and gentry. This provided a platform of economic support for the action. The political support came from the publication of Cromwell's initial report via a series of leaks to Ye Olde Currant Bun*. The resulting headlines were all the sort you might expect: monks drunk at mass, nuns having it away with each other and/or getting pregnant with the monks, abbots fathering up to six children, corruption involving the illegal selling of timber, and an unnatural interest in choirboys. The whole affair became a bit like a Ken Russell* fantasy.

Despite the propaganda onslaught, there was some resistance to Henry's measures, with armed uprisings in Lincolnshire, Yorkshire, and, later, Norfolk. The Pilgrimage of Grace, as the Yorkshire uprising was known, was defeated by a mixture of overwhelming force and the offer of amnesty by Bluff King Hal's men, which, naturally enough, was reneged on. The King did, however, keep his word and came up with a pension for the monks and nuns who cooperated with his plans. In 1538, everything was just beginning to calm down when the Pope stuck his oar in by excommunicating Henry. Henry retaliated by annexing the larger monasteries that were not originally part of the plan. The result was that, by 1540, all eight hundred fifty nunneries and monastic houses in the country had been taken over and had their assets liquidated.

Mr. Horner is mentioned in another rhyme that alludes to the transfer of this monastic land to the gentry:

Hopton, Horner, Smyth and Thynne
When the abbots went out, they came in.

So Henry got a lot of land that was cheaply distributed to up-and-coming gentry such as Mr. Horner, as well as a colossal amount of gold plate, jewellery, and all manner of other trinkets. This was clearly useful for a man who famously had a habit of upgrading wives every few years. Not that he went in much for maintenance payments. Finally, where does this leave the Horner family? Well, the last time anybody checked, they were still living in Mells Manor.

Jack Be Nimble

Jack be nimble, Jack be quick,
Jack jumped over a candlestick.

Various pagan associations here, with fortune-telling, fertility, and it being considered good luck to be able to jump over a candlestick without the flame going out. The ability to do this meant a prosperous year ahead. For no apparent reason, Buckinghamshire was once a real hot spot for candle leaping and even elevated it to a sport, which, considering some current Olympic "events," is probably a reasonable thing to do. The lacemakers of Wendover used to practise it on the feast of their patron saint, St. Catherine, 25 November.

Perhaps if you were nimble enough to clear the flame, it meant you were a lean and healthy person up for the challenges of the year ahead, whereas the lardier among the crowd might cause a draught and put the fire out. Maybe it was some early management test to assess the aptness of

31

workers for the job, with those who put out the fire being laid off. This could certainly be thought of as bad luck.

Before you dismiss what's being said as a flight of fancy, just run your mind over some of the absurd management-training courses and aptitude tests currently in vogue. In comparison, jumping over a candlestick is quick, cost-effective, and would probably yield better results. In fact, a book called *The Pagan Way to Human Resource Management* would surely be a great success. Chapter headings by guest authors could include one by the Druids on sacrifice, one by followers of Zeus and the Hellenic tradition on bull markets, and maybe a piece by the followers of Osiris and the Egyptian pantheon on pyramid selling.

There are happier links for this rhyme in pre-Christian fertility rituals involving jumping over fire and some, perhaps more sensible, young couples today still "jump the broomstick." Fire jumping for fertility is one of the ceremonies shown in the film *The Wicker Man*, which concerns pagan religious beliefs on a Scottish island in the last century. Those who have seen the film might remember the divinity lessons that consisted of naked girls leaping over fire in order to promote their fecundity. When the policeman from the mainland (played by Edward Woodward) objects to the girls' nakedness, Lord Summerisle (Christopher Lee) points out that it would be much too dangerous with their clothes on. To those of you who have not seen *The Wicker Man*, it's really time you did.

It's falling down
London Bridge

London Bridge is falling down,
falling down, falling down.
London Bridge is falling down,
my fair lady.

Build it up with wood and clay,
wood and clay, wood and clay.
Wood and clay will wash away,
my fair lady.

Build it up with iron bars,
iron bars, iron bars.
Iron bars will bend and bow, my fair lady.

Build it up with silver and gold,
silver and gold, silver and gold.
Silver and gold will be stole away,
my fair lady.[†]

[†]There are a number of additional verses that may be added here including the lines "get a man to watch all night" and "get a dog to bark all night." However, these solutions to the bridge's problems meet with challenges of their own: the man falls asleep and the dog finds a bone. Nothing works until the bridge is made of stone.

Build it up with strongest stone,
strongest stone, strongest stone.
Strongest stone will last alone,
my fair lady.

"London Bridge" is most likely based on a Norwegian poem by Ottar Svarte, celebrating the victory of King Olav (also a saint in Norway) in alliance with the English King Aethelred (Unready Eddie) against the invading Danes. Olav, whose reward is a street named after him near the current bridge, Tooley Street (if you swap the "Y" for a "V" and add an "S" at the front, it makes sense), cannily attached his ships to the wooden London Bridge and waited for the tide so he could tow the bridge away. The poem itself, which loses a bit in the translation, goes like this:

London Bridge is broken down,
Gold is won and bright renown.
Shields resounding, war horns
   sounding,
Hildur shouting in the din!
Arrows singing, mail coats ringing,
Odin makes our Olav win!
King Aethelred has found a friend,
Brave Olav will his throne defend,

In bloody fight maintain his right,
Win back his land with blood-red hand,
And Aethelred's son on his throne
    replace —
Edmund, the star of every royal race.

Except that the Danes didn't like
Edmund (Aethelred's son) and chose to
back Cnut (Canute), who sneakily, after
the Norwegians had gone home, took their
fleet south of the bridge site by means of a
huge channel. After defeating Edmund, the
Danes split the kingdom and indeed
London itself into Danish and Saxon parts.
Anyway, that's all very interesting but has
nothing to do with the nursery rhyme,
which appears to be based on the Olav victory poem but extended to celebrate the
new stone bridge.

The meaning of the "new" rhyme is a bit
obvious but worth exploring for the story
of the bridge itself. The rhyme is both a
celebration of the most famous London
bridge and a comment on the failure of its
predecessors. The bridge in the rhyme was
completed in the thirteenth century and
lasted six hundred years. In 1832, it was
replaced by a gorgeous bridge built by
John Rennie and then subsequently by the
drab slab hastily erected in 1973 a little

way upstream of the original sites. The rhyme recognizes that the six-hundred-year-old bridge required constant maintenance against the forces of Thames and tide, as it was always being rebuilt over the period. But it did stand the test of time, even if the maintenance of it went on for ever, in much the same way as the rhyme can go on for ever (remember those additional verses).

Previous bridges had been a bit short-term. There had been a Roman bridge of wood and a succession of new bridges between the tenth and twelfth centuries, including the one that Olav memorably towed away. So the stone bridge, which took thirty-three years to build and had a road twenty feet wide and three hundred yards long, was a real step forward, a wonder of the world. In 1209, the bridge had twenty arches, each sixty feet high and thirty feet wide, with twenty feet between each arch. There was a tower and a gate at both the northern and southern ends of the bridge. Beyond the south tower and gate there was a wooden drawbridge to prevent an invasion of London from that direction. There were shops, houses, and even a chapel on it. It was a scene of lavish celebrations and jousting tournaments.

Traitors' heads were displayed on spears there, a fact cheerfully commemorated by a giant white spike on the current bridge. The bridge was a bit of a hazard and, aside from death by spike to the head, parts of it frequently fell off and there were a number of disastrous fires. A consequence was that many people died on or near the bridge, including a boatload of Jews travelling to exile after their expulsion by Edward I in 1290. They drowned in the rapids caused by the bridge's narrow arches, and apparently their ghosts still haunt the north shore, not far from where the monument to the Fire of London stands today.

These rapids and the actions of the tide are the reason the current bridge stands one hundred or so feet to the west of the original ones. John Rennie's 1832 bridge was destabilized by the tides that had previously been held in check by the tight arches of the six-hundred-year-old bridge. Once free of these constrictions, the Thames undermined Rennie's bridge much more swiftly than anyone had anticipated. Its move to the US piece by piece, where it is now positioned in a park at Lake Havasu City, Arizona (originally without water, the lake was created for it to span), was a wonderful feat of organization and engineering, and takes some beating for sheer eccentricity. The current bridge, in contrast, is more of a monument to early 1970s functionalism and has little to recommend it. For the definitive account of London Bridge, read Patricia Pierce's *Old London Bridge.*

Except that she doesn't mention the human sacrifices. It was apparently customary in the long ago and far away to secure a building or bridge through sacrifice to the dcities of the area or river. The preferred offering involved children, their blood, or, if possible, the sealing in of a child with a candle and hunk of bread at the foot of the bridge. When the Bridge Gate at Bremen was demolished in the nineteenth century, the skeleton of a child was indeed found implanted in the foundations. Nor are songs about bridges falling down unique to Britain, with examples coming from Italy, France, and Germany. The idea behind the sacrifice was that the spirit of the youngster looked over the bridge using the light and stayed awake by eating the food.

In Romania it was believed that the sacrifice of a person's shadow to a building or bridge would do the trick. People would be enticed to stand over the foundation and their shadow measured. This written measurement was then buried with the foundation stone. Sadly, it was also believed that the person whose shadow was buried in such a fashion would die within forty days of the building's completion. So-called "shadow traders" still existed in Eastern Europe until the nineteenth century, and people would shout out warnings to those passing freshly erected buildings to beware in case someone stole their shadow. These are interesting, if gruesome, legends, but there is scant evidence linking London Bridge specifically to such practices.

"Rivers and child sacrifice," you might scoff. "Dark Ages stuff!" Except that in the twenty-first century such practices still take place. On 21 September 2001, the headless torso of a young boy was found floating near Tower Bridge. He had been used as part of something called a muti ceremony, in which the body parts of a child are used for medicinal purposes or to bring good fortune to a business enterprise. Police throughout Europe believe that there have been perhaps a dozen such cases across the Continent in the last few years, even though this particular variant of mumbo-jumbo is Southern African in origin.

Who let them out?

Hark, Hark, the Dogs Do Bark

Hark, hark, the dogs do bark,
The beggars are coming to town;
Some in rags,
And some in jags,
And one in a velvet gown.

"Hark, Hark" is basically saying, "Listen to the dogs — they're warning of the arrival of beggars and other ne'er-do-wells in our town." Today, the barking dogs might quite possibly belong to the beggars themselves and, if certain government ministers are to be believed, the panhandlers would also possess velvet gowns and arrive in Jags (E-types, most likely) before setting up shop to separate innocent citizens from their money.

One thread of explanation is that the rhyme refers to roaming bands of beggars in the Elizabethan era, when the first vagrancy, or vagabond, laws were passed. An act of 1572 stated that vagabonds were to be whipped, then "branded through the gristle of the right ear with an inch-thick hot iron." The enclosure of agricultural land, as well as the break-up and selling off of Church lands by Henry VIII in the 1530s, caused many people to lose their homes or access to land that they once shared. In both town and countryside, more people were competing for limited resources but, because the population was concentrated into a smaller space in the built-up areas, there was a greater opportunity for crime and begging. Traditional forms of relief from the parishes failed to cope with the situation, and the government authorities also found it hard to control.

Fear of the mob or roving bands of mendicants is a common theme throughout European history, and it doesn't matter whether these are religiously inspired rabbles, criminal syndicates, landless peasants, or gypsy travellers — in effect, the rhyme fits anyone who disturbs the peace of a settled town. A glance through today's newspapers would show that not much has changed. In some cases, the fear of beggars is a cover for prejudiced behaviour against anyone who is different ("the other"), and folklore from across the world abounds with tales of strangers arriving in towns, bringing chaos in their wake. There are, however, just as many about gods turning up disguised as visitors and exacting revenge on uncharitable hosts.

That was a roundabout way of saying that the rhyme has a fairly universal theme and could be used to describe any time from the Middle Ages to the present day. Having said that, the first-known written version of a song which bears any resemblance to it has no mention of scroungers at all:

> Hark, hark, the dogs do bark,
> My wife is coming in.
> With rogues and jades,
> And roaring blades,
> They make a devilish din.

Here is the tale of a chap sitting quietly at home, perhaps with his pipe and slippers, bemoaning the fact that his wife has been out on the razzle* (and, for all he knows, appearing in it). She comes in from her night out, with a series of shouty fellows to wreck her husband's peace. This particular rhyme appeared in something called the *Westminster Drollery* in 1672 and it is unclear whether it is a reworking of an earlier rhyme about beggars or whether the rhyme about beggars is based on this one. This is important because, if the latter is the case, there could be some truth to the theory that the rhyme is actually about William of Orange (William III), who finally defeated James II in 1690 to complete his capture of the crown. On the other hand, if the beggars' rhyme predates William's accession, then the rhyme could not have been written about him but could plausibly have become associated with him at the time. William apparently is the one with the velvet gown and the others are his Dutch followers. It's possible that supporters of James saw him as a beggar pleading for the crown, but, in reality, many people in Britain actively encouraged William to claim the throne, and certainly when he arrived in the country he received a great deal of support. This enabled him fairly quickly to rout James's armies in mainland Britain and later in Ireland. The term "beggar" was used to describe the Dutch in the seventeenth century but, even so, William's rule was not associated with financial imprudence or pleading for resources. Furthermore, while Britain did have issues with the Dutch (four trade wars from 1652 to 1684, with breaks for recuperating and recovering from bouts of the Black Death), they were never great enemies like, say, the French, the Spanish, or, later, the Germans. There were not, for example, a sprinkling of anti-Dutch pubs across London, whereas there were pubs named "Antigallican," meaning "against the French."

So if the rhyme is not specifically an anti-Dutch affair, it brings us back to the other meaning, that of a generalized warning about beggars coming to town. If you throw in the additional verse below, most contemporary responses to beggars appear to be taken care of — except for the times when you hide your face and look away or offer them a cigarette instead of money:

Some people gave them white bread,
Some people gave them brown,
And some gave them a good horse whip,
And sent them out of town.

Or you could just walk on by, like Sir George Young, the ex–housing minister, who is probably not the first person to describe homeless beggars as "the sort of people you step over when you come out of the opera." Presumably it wasn't John Gay's *Beggar's Opera* he had been to see, even if it has been packing them in since 1728. Many of the finest minds of the eighteenth and nineteenth centuries turned their attention to the problem of vagrancy, including Jonathan Swift and Charles Babbage (father of the computer), who wrote a study on the problems of begging, as have other bright sparks before and since.

A series of legislative measures was enacted against new age travellers at the end of the twentieth century and anti-begging exclusion orders were introduced in the twenty-first. Whether aggressive, organized, or just desperate, the beggar seems to be a feature of human life, forever with us, from the King of the Beggars of twelfth-century London (William Longbeard) to the pushy, pin-eyed panhandlers of today. One clear difference between the world of begging in the rhyme and now, though, is that if today's dogs become too dangerous, they can be destroyed. Unless they're royal — then they just get put into therapy.

Fancy a rub-a-dub, then, matey?

Rub-a-Dub-Dub

Rub-a-dub-dub,
Three men in a tub,
And how do you think they got there?
The butcher, the baker,
the candlestick-maker,
They all jumped out of a rotten potato,
'Twas enough to make a man stare.

The world of nursery rhymes is crying out for positive images of homosexuality, and you would bet that this verse is surely about Chariots Sauna in Shoreditch or some other bathhouse. Sadly, no. In fact, it's strange, but there seems to be a paucity of gay rhymes. There are plenty about men having fun together, and lots, like this example, with double entendre potential, but nothing much doing for gay men. Nothing doing either for Rastafarians in this dub* one. In fact, racism is pleasingly absent from most of the English rhymes, except when it comes to having a pop at the Welsh or Scots.

It really wouldn't do, having raised the prurient possibility of man-on-man hot, steamy action in nursery rhymes, to leave you entirely dissatisfied. So you will be relieved to know that it is based on another rhyme, which goes like this:

Hey! Rub-a-dub! Ho! Rub-a-dub!
    Three maids in a tub,
And who do you think were there?
The butcher, the baker, the
    candlestick-maker,
And all of them gone to the fair!

Clearly we are talking peep show here. Just possibly they might have joined the maids for an assisted rub in the tub later. A group of respectable tradesmen caught out at a naughty fair sideshow is something the British still take a delight in to this day. Though, naturally, the strip joints of long ago were likely to be much more sensibly named than those of today. The Bawdy Strumpet or Reeling Saucy Trollops would certainly be more appealing names than the anodyne stupidity of Spearmint Rhino, plus I bet the complimentary matchboxes were more interesting then too.

Goosie, Goosie, Gander

Goosie, goosie, gander,
Where shall I wander?
Upstairs and downstairs,
And in my lady's chamber.

There I met an old man,
Who wouldn't say his prayers.
So I took him by the left leg,
And threw him down the stairs.

Well, it's nothing to do with geese — of the feathered variety, at least. Although, interestingly, one theory has it that the "old man" is a daddy-long-legs and the last verse is about children picking the legs off him — either as a cruel game of "he loves me, he loves me not" or as an exercise in home pest-control. Much more attention-grabbing, though, is to follow the route that, in days gone by, "goose" was a common term for prostitute.

Some of the most famous of these were the Winchester Geese, from Southwark in south London, where licensed brothels existed from the Middle Ages. Henry II had actually set them up with royal protection and also owned a chain in Cherbourg. Some historians, however, date the "stews" (brothels) near the Thames as far back as Roman times, whether operating with or without royal approval.

To be "bitten by a goose," and suffer the consequent swellings caused by venereal disease, was a common complaint, with "goose bumps" being as prevalent among the dissolute wealthy as among the urban poor. When Henry VIII had the brothels closed in Southwark, an order reinforced by his daughter Elizabeth I, it caused the "geese" to disperse to the theatres and streets. The brothels were not closed without some difficulty, including sieges and all manner of resistance. So it was not until one hundred years later, in 1650, that prostitution and Southwark ceased to be synonymous when the theatres were closed during Cromwell's Commonwealth. Cromwell's shutting of the theatres drove away the crowds, which in turn meant that there was limited patronage for the good-time girls. All that happened, of course, was that the toms reassembled around the new theatre district of Covent Garden, leaving

50

Southwark to years of decline until its rein-carnation as Art and Museum Central in contemporary London.

So the early part of the rhyme conceivably alludes to the spread of venereal disease. It was everywhere, even in a "lady's chamber." The use of "lady" could be ironic here, but who knows? As the Church owned the land on which the brothels stood in the sixteenth century, part of the reason for their closure was that the brothels represented in some respects the old Catholic way of doing things. Shutting the stews was really about taking Church land. When Henry VIII took the land, he also took the power from the bishops, particularly the Bishop of Winchester, who controlled much of the land in Southwark. Morality had little to do with the King's action (revenge might, as some sources claim that he had the pox himself), although it was presented in that light at the time. Pleasingly for Henry, the fact that the land the brothels stood on was controlled by the Bishop created a link between venereal disease and Catholicism. In the second part of the rhyme, the "old man" possibly represents the (old) Catholic religion. "Not saying your prayers" could then refer to the *New English Prayer Book*, which was published for the Church of England by Archbishop Cranmer. This prayer book was in English rather than Latin and was promoted quite firmly by the Protestant authorities. Catholics refused to use it and would therefore be punished. Finally, "left leg" (or "left-footer") is an English term for Catholics, who were quite rigorously suppressed during Edward VI's reign and later that of Elizabeth I. So there you have the rhyme complete.

Back to Southwark and its redevelopment this century. One of the sites being worked on is the former Cross Bones cemetery at the junction of Redcross Way and Union Street in London SE1.* This was formerly a graveyard that is popularly believed to be Europe's only prostitute burial ground. John Stow, in his *Survey of London* (1603), described the burial site as being "dedicated to single women forbidden the rites of the Church so long as they continued a sinful life." Little is left of the original cemetery. It was built over in Victorian times and, more recently, burrowed under for the Jubilee Line tube* extension. In view of the fact that London SE1 already has more museums per square foot than anywhere else in the world, however, this should surely be the spot for a museum to the "geese" that initially made Southwark famous.

Piecing together the story
Humpty-Dumpty

Humpty-Dumpty sat on a wall,
Humpty-Dumpty had a great fall.
All the King's horses
and all the King's men,
Couldn't put Humpty together again.

There's fun to be had with this rhyme. The *Oxford English Dictionary* describes a "humpty-dumpty" as "an ale-and-brandy-based drink or a clumsy person of either sex." The rhyme has echoes across Europe, being called "Boule Boule" in France and "Thille Lille" in Sweden, for example. The story in each place is the same, though: Egg sits on wall; egg falls from wall; egg smashes.

Both the universality of the rhyme and its theme suggest that it is very old, which lends itself to a neat psychoanalytical explanation. The association of eggs and falling and things never being the same again might have something to do with unlooked-for pregnancy. Other, deeper, analysts see the egg as a motif for mankind, representing the essential fragility of the human condition, while in some cultures the egg symbolizes the soul. This is all well and happy as a means of explaining the roots of the rhyme, but there is an eggstra-ordinary twist to this tale, at least according to another theory.

Apart from being the name of a drink and a means of referring to an ungainly person, "Humpty-Dumpty" was also the name given to a huge and powerful cannon that stood on the walls of Colchester. At least, that's the tale from the East Anglia tourist board — the local museum in Colchester is more sceptical.

The story goes that, during the English Civil War (1642–49), Humpty was mounted on top of the wall of St. Mary's Church in Colchester. In common with other cannons of the time, it was made of cast iron. Now, while cast iron is not as light as an egg, it is nevertheless quite brittle and shatters if mishandled.

The city of Colchester — a Parliamentarian[*] (Roundhead) stronghold — had been captured by Royalists (Cavaliers) in 1648. It might be fair to deduce from this that, as a defensive fixture, Humpty can't have been all that great. The King's men held on to the city for eleven weeks and, during the Parliamentarian counter-siege, decided to use Humpty against the Parliamentarians. Unfortunately, they lacked the skill to fire Humpty-Dumpty properly and managed to blow the cannon to pieces. (In an alternative version the enemy hit the church tower.) Either way, Humpty-Dumpty was left in pieces all over the ground and "all the King's horses and all the King's men couldn't put Humpty together again." So here is a case of an ancient folk rhyme being given new life as an anti-Royalist chant. It might, at this juncture, be interesting to trace when people started using the words "Roundhead" and "Cavalier" to describe whether a man has been circumcised or not, but that really is a separate issue.

Sing a Song of Sixpence

Sing a song of sixpence,
A pocket full of rye,
Four and twenty blackbirds,
Baked in a pie.
When the pie was opened,
The birds began to sing,
Now, wasn't that a dainty dish
To set before the King?

The King was in his counting house,
Counting out his money.
The Queen was in the parlour,
Eating bread and honey.
The maid was in the garden,
Hanging out the clothes.
When along came a blackbird,
And snipped off her nose!

Alternative theories abound for this one, but first a little culinary history. Once upon a time apparently, people baked little clay whistles into the pastry on the top of pies. These whistles were shaped like the heads of birds with their beaks wide open. The idea was that when the pie was cut and the crust broken, the cold air outside met the hot contents inside, creating lots of steam. The steam would then rise up through the whistles, making the "birds' heads" appear to sing. Also, the eating of songbirds was considered normal in England, and still is in parts of Italy, so if blackbirds were considered to be a culinary delicacy, then they were fit for royal consumption. Therefore, the whole thing could just be about a meal, simple as that. All sorts of creatures were put in pies in the past, although the notion of people jumping out of food dishes did not come along until the reign of Queen Anne.

According to the leading theory, this rhyme is about Henry VIII and two of his six wives: the maid hanging out the washing in the garden is Anne Boleyn, blissfully unaware of her future loss of head and status, and the Queen is Catherine of Aragon, mother of Mary Tudor.

As with "Little Jack Horner," the business about the pie is related to the dissolution of the monasteries. Nowadays many "crusties" take jobs as cycle couriers, but in the past there was a real crusty courier service whereby valuable documents were hidden in pies (and other everyday objects) in order to conceal their worth from brigands. The story goes that King Henry VIII had the deeds to yet more monasteries concealed in a pie that was sent to him. The King's men went to the monasteries to open them up and persuade the "blackbirds" there (clergymen were often jokingly associated with blackbirds, as nuns are associated with penguins today) to sing — that is, to "sing" in the more modern (Mafia, if you like) sense, meaning to plead and betray. Some monks tried to advance themselves by grassing up* the abbot, who may have hidden a few items from the King's men — little things like gold crosses and ruby-encrusted mitres, valuable things that would cause even a monarch to reassess his cash value.

So the King is in the counting house. Queen Catherine is out of the way in the parlour, divorced from the action. Ms. Boleyn waits in the garden and finds all her new-found riches come to an abrupt end with her beheading. Elements of the clergy (those blackbirds again) are also getting their own back with accusations of witchcraft against her. In real life Anne got to choose her own executioner, a

Frenchman, and is quoted as having said, "I hear he's quite good and I have a very small neck!" She also referred to herself in the tower as "Queen Lackhead," which has to be the epitome of gallows humour.

The whole break with the Church of Rome, and the dissolution of the monasteries, came about as a result of the divorce of Catherine for Anne. It is perhaps a shame that the rhyme doesn't go on to chronicle what happened to the other wives. For that we have "Divorced, beheaded, died; divorced, beheaded, survived" as a handy mnemonic to remind us of their fates.

Mary, Mary, Quite Contrary

Mary, Mary, quite contrary,
How does your garden grow?
With silver bells and cockle-shells,
And pretty maids all in a row.

It seems fairly clear that this rhyme is about someone called Mary — all about Mary, you could say. Whether it is Mary mother of God, Mary Queen of Scots, Mary Tudor, or any old Mary is a matter of some debate. Those who believe that it might be a description of Our Lady's convent link the "bells" to the Sanctus bells and the "cockle-shells" to the badges worn by pilgrims. The "pretty maids" would be the nuns in the service of Mary. This Catholic interpretation of the rhyme fits quite nicely with the notion that it could refer to other, more temporal Marys who were involved in the succession to Henry VIII of England and had powerful Protestant enemies.

Mary Tudor, Henry's daughter, took the throne and was followed by Elizabeth I, while Mary Queen of Scots attempted to claim the throne instead of Elizabeth and failed. Both Marys were Catholic, one closely allied to Spain (Mary Tudor) and the other to France (Mary Queen of Scots). One of the latter Mary's links to the rhyme is the fact that her lifestyle angered Protestant ministers in Scotland. The "silver bells" are real flowers but in this case might allude to her wealth and liking for fancy trinkets. "Cockle-shells" are a type of shellfish and the line may just be referring to a fondness for seafood or to shells as a means of making a garden more decorative. Interestingly, Mary Queen of Scots had four ladies in waiting also called Mary, the "Four Marys." These were nothing like the nice young girls who used to appear in the comic *Bunty*,* but they could explain the "pretty maids all in a row."

More salaciously, the line might be a reference to cuckolded husbands whose wives were attracted to the Frenchmen at Mary's court, these wives being the "pretty maids all in a row." It seems that Mary's court was full of individuals who enjoyed beautiful things, whether this meant attractive objects or gorgeous people, and that everyone at court was having a fine old time. What we appear to have is a gripe from some Puritan Scotch folk about other people enjoying themselves. Nothing too serious, and in this context it is worth remembering something P. G. Wodehouse said about it being "never difficult to tell the difference between a ray of sunshine and a Scotsman with a grievance."

There is a more sombre theory that, although the rhyme is a Protestant condemnation of Mary Queen of Scots, it is not about her lifestyle choices but rather the life choices that she imposed on others. That Mary was "quite contrary" would mean she was duplicitous and unpredictable. The "garden" referred to is Scotland, which is a cemetery that grows full with the graves of Protestant martyrs. The "silver bells and cockle-shells" are sideways references to instruments of torture (thumbscrews and the like), and the "pretty maids all in a row" are the women left widowed by Mary's executioners.

If this last theory is correct, the Mary in this rhyme could just as well be Mary Tudor, alias "Bloody Mary." (It would be interesting to know if the drink and the card game are named after her as well.)

During her short reign, after Henry's son Edward VI and before Elizabeth I, she ruthlessly set about a counter-reformation, burning and torturing Protestants. So the same explanation as above, but England rather than Scotland. Perhaps Mary Queen of Scots should get this rhyme, though, as Mary Tudor also has connections with "Three Blind Mice."

It's likely that the rhyme has come to represent either Mary, depending on how it's interpreted. However, lack of a written version of the rhyme in its current form before the eighteenth century does make proving association very difficult. There is a much earlier rhyme that contains the line "Sing! Cuckolds all in a row," which this one appears linked to and which fits nicely with the notion of the cuckolded husbands in Mary Queen of Scots' court. So the cast-iron proof is not there but it is easier to believe any of the above than that the rhyme is about some prototype Charlie Dimmock.* For a start, if that were the case, where's the water feature?

A short tale?

Three Blind Mice

Three blind mice,
Three blind mice.
See how they run!
See how they run!
They all ran after the farmer's wife,
Who cut off their tails with a carving knife,
Did you ever see such a thing in your life?
As three blind mice.

Mary Tudor, the daughter of Henry VIII and his first wife, Catherine of Aragon, is thought by some to be the farmer's wife in this rhyme. Half Spanish herself, Mary also married a Spaniard, Philip, thinking to strengthen an alliance that had worked well for her father. Mary was keen to reinstate Catholicism as the religion of England after years during which first her father and then, in a far more ruthless fashion, her half brother Edward had attempted to stamp it out. Parliament was contrite enough and apologized for all the anti-papal legislation it had passed, but many of the people and nobility were not so willing to submit.

Mary came to power with popular backing to end the nine-day reign of Lady Jane Grey, who had been hastily installed on the throne to keep the succession Protestant. As the eldest daughter of Henry, Mary was a popular choice but, in the twenty years since Henry had divorced Mary's mother, England had changed dramatically. Both Spain and the Catholic Church were regarded with deep suspicion and, while armed rebellion was quickly extinguished, many Protestants refused to abandon their faith. So Mary decided to burn it out of them, largely, it should be added, from frustration at their obstinacy.

Several of the victims were high-profile political opponents, but many were ordinary people. Treason against the Queen was obviously a crime, as was defying the Catholic authorities, but so was reading the Bible in English. Among those who disobeyed this prohibition were some blind folk — Joan Waste and John Aprice are two whose names are recorded. They had saved up to buy the Bible in English and have it read to them. However, it is unclear why these blind mice (both literally blind and serving as a symbol for insignificant people in general) have their tails cut off in the rhyme rather than being burned (what actually happened).

At Lewes in East Sussex, a bonfire is held every year to commemorate these and other Protestant martyrs. On 5 November the whole town dresses up to represent different periods of the town's history and, at the "Cliffe Bonfire," a huge effigy of the Pope is burned alongside two other people deemed to be enemies of the bonfire. These can be local or national politicians, or even international figures. In the past they have included Margaret Thatcher, Ronald Reagan, and Princess Anne among others.

Britain's history was scarred by disputes between Catholics and Protestants even before the break with Rome and the dissolution of the monasteries in the 1530s. For two hundred years after that there were struggles for power and supremacy between the two. In the Middle Ages, movements like the Lollards* had demanded a more accountable Church and had been suppressed. There were other forms of religious persecution too. The Jews suffered terribly across Europe and were expelled from England in 1290 by Edward I. If witchcraft is considered a religion, then even more religious minorities were squashed metaphorically, even if actual "trial by pressing" was outlawed in the thirteenth century. Waves of religious migrants left Britain (and elsewhere in Europe) to settle in the Americas in order to practise their religion in peace. Practice, of course, makes perfect, and the United States is now home to some of the most fanatical Christians on the planet.

Paradoxically, as the rule of law and democracy of sorts developed in Britain from the seventeenth century on, the country became a haven for people who had been persecuted elsewhere — Protestant groups from mainland Europe in particular, the Huguenots being perhaps the most famous example. In later years, thousands of Jews moved to Britain and the rather irreligious nature of the British from the eighteenth century onwards seems to have helped them settle. Perhaps because of the carnage of the post-Tudor years, British people realized that religion was dangerous stuff and the best approach was to create a benign version that offended no one. The Church of England is unlikely to unleash jihads because its rallying cry (which Eddie Izzard* paraphrased as "Tea and cakes or death") is unlikely to whip up much of a frenzy. Interestingly, Izzard himself is a descendant of French migrants. Who says immigrants don't enrich our culture?

Britain now has one of the lowest rates of church attendance in the world, and this has been the case since the mid-Victorian era. Yet British people still define themselves by their religion if asked. Amusingly, according to the 2001 census, the *Star Wars* religion of Jedi makes up 0.7 per cent of the population, while Christians account for 72 per cent and Muslims 3 per cent. Jedi therefore outnumber the 329,000 Sikhs, 260,000 Jews, and 144,000 Buddhists who filled in forms. British society could therefore be described as a broad church, even if most of us don't actually visit one very often.

A child's guide to taxation
Baa, Baa, Black Sheep

Baa, baa, black sheep, have you any wool?
Yes, sir, yes, sir, three bags full.
One for the master, one for the dame,
And one for the little boy
who lives down the lane.

"Baa, Baa, Black Sheep" is an early complaint about taxes. Some versions even end, "And none for the little boy who lives down the lane," which seems very unfair, as the "little boy" represented either the farmers or the people of England.

The wealth of England was largely a result of the trade in wool, hence the "woolsack" on which the Lord Chancellor still sits today in the House of Lords. The woolsack was introduced by King Edward III in the fourteenth century and though originally filled with English wool, it is currently packed with wool from each of the countries of the Commonwealth, in order to express unity among member states. Quite how a British lord plonking himself down on the produce of more than fifty countries symbolizes concord is hard to say, though it does provide a good metaphor for the British Empire.

During feudal times, taxes did not go to the Chancellor or even the European Union. In the Middle Ages, farmers were required to give one-third of their income (which could be in the form of goods such as wool) to their "master" — the local lord — who would in turn pass one-third of it to the King, and another third to the "dame" (representing the Church). The final third they kept for themselves or sold, and this was the part that went to the "little boy." Of course, if you really want to bleat about it, the sheep started off with all the wool but ended up with none at all.

Maybe having your wool nicked is a better fate than that which befell black sheep in areas of East Africa. There, during times of no rain, they were placed on the roof of a hut and had their stomachs slit open and the contents hurled about, all in order to promote rainfall. This is perhaps why sheep like Wales and Yorkshire so much: with the constant rain, they stand a reasonable chance of never being sacrificed, whatever other indignities they may be forced to suffer.

Grand Old
Duke of York

Oh, the grand old Duke of York,
He had ten thousand men.
He marched them up to the top of the hill,
And he marched them down again.
And when they were up, they were up.
And when they were down,
they were down.
And when they were only halfway up,
They were neither up nor down.

As the English monarch's second child has long borne the title of Duke of York, in theory any younger son of a monarch who led an army could fit the profile of the subject of this rhyme. The ditty was definitely, though inaccurately, used by a contemporary journalist about Frederick, Duke of York, to describe his campaign in Flanders against Napoleon. Inaccurately, because Frederick did not climb any hills in his campaign and Flanders is notoriously flat.

Nevertheless, the point of the journalist's skit was to poke fun at this particular Duke of York's lack of military talents.

So it's used about Frederick, but the rhyme is based on an earlier song used about the King of France ("The Brave Old King of France Had 40,000 Men"), concocted during one of the lapses in the centuries-long feuding between England and France. So it predates Frederick and can be seen as generic, a sort of proto football chant used to taunt your enemy as a clueless military leader. It was just a question of changing the words slightly in order to direct the abuse at your chosen target.

Although the association is now fairly firmly fixed on Frederick, there are theories that it had also been applied to a previous Duke of York. This was the man who eventually became King James II and who lost the throne over his failure to face up to William of Orange. Had it been James I, the phrase "had 10,000 men" might have occasioned a whole new meaning in view of his intimate relationship with the Duke of Buckingham (see "Georgy Porgy").

When applied to James II, the rhyme refers to the occasion when William of Orange landed in England, intent on ousting James, and the King marched his troops to

Salisbury Plain to face the invaders. When he discovered that many English leaders (including his former ally the powerful landowner John Churchill, later Duke of Marlborough) had defected to William's side, James ordered his troops to retreat ("marched them down again"). The whole exercise was evidently pointless, hence the rhyme's statement of the bleeding obvious. It should be said that James was not too bad as a fighter — he was just an inept leader. Having surrendered to the Parliamentary forces in the Civil War, he went on to gain military experience abroad during his own and his brother's time in exile while Cromwell was in office.

James was, in many ways, a pivotal monarch in British history. He was a suspicious character who lacked the charm and good looks of his brother Charles II, although his troubles really began only after his conversion to Catholicism. James had run-ins with Parliament, which tried to ban his succession as a Catholic, but it was his crushing of the rebellion led by his brother's (illegitimate) son, the Duke of Monmouth, in 1685 that really turned people against him — not so much because of the defeat of the Duke but because of the retribution that followed.

These events also established the reputation of James's ally Judge Jeffreys, otherwise known as the Hanging Judge. It's hard to imagine a nastier character than Jeffreys, a drink-sodden, sharp-witted social climber with the morals of a rattlesnake. No doubt his talents would be in great demand today as a media commentator or spin-doctor. After the defeat of Monmouth's army by John Churchill, Jeffreys conducted a series of show trials known as the Bloody Assizes in retribution for the rebellion. The free hand given to Jeffreys by James and the latter's failure to see the consequences of letting a madman like Jeffreys loose ensured that his judgement and his religion counted against him.

This general lack of foresight was typical of James, who ended his reign fleeing across the Thames and throwing the great seal of office (sadly, not the animal but a stamp for impressing wax) into the Thames. He believed that without this symbol of authority William would be unable to govern. The action was futile as a London fisherman pulled the seal out of the river a few days later. James was not done yet, though, and tried to rally the Catholics of Britain against William. He started his campaign in Ireland and marched on Derry/Londonderry, only to be locked out of the city by a bunch of Protestant apprentice boys after the city elders had negotiated surrender with him. This was the turning point in his attempt to reclaim the throne, and he was eventually defeated by William's (King Billy's) army at the battle of the Boyne on 12 July 1690.

This event still rumbles down in song and chant today at football matches and on the streets of Scotland and Northern Ireland, and it is in many ways at the root of the current political situation in the province. And all because one leader could lead his troops while another couldn't. James's reign is also behind much of the legislation banning a Catholic succession to the throne. Mind you, New York was named after him (replacing Peter Stuyvesant's New Amsterdam), so it would be unfair to say he had an entirely wasted life.

A Frog He Would a-Wooing Go

There are a number of themes running through nursery rhymes about courtship and marriage that are peculiarly English. These include the element of personal choice and the frank admission that the English marriage is a marketplace, a trade-off if you will. Generally, the man offers the goods and the woman the good looks, but there are a few exceptions and no shortage of pretty boys in the nursery-rhyme world. Choice of partner is central to many rhymes, and several warn about what could happen if a poor selection is made. The sensible Welsh preferred to carry on with a practice known as "bundling." This was a prenuptial trial which left the two lovebirds tied up together in a giant sack overnight and encouraged them to do whatever came naturally. The logic behind it was that if the couple were still on speaking terms after the experience, the marriage was set fair. If they were not, well, they'd had a good night romping around in something woolly, so no great loss there.

In some rhymes the fear of women is projected. Contrasted with the good, nurturing mother is the rapacious whore who will drag a good man down, or even to his death. Apparently, though, if you wish to get Freudian about it, all men fear that the one who has given life may also take it away. The next rhyme concerns the pull of the two women in a young man's life and the fatal results of eating eel pie with the wrong one. Eels are a classic phallic symbol and, in this context, the eating of this dish represents castration and death. At the very least, it could represent the death of the child who has now become a man and consequently must leave his mother:

Where have you been to, Billy my
  son?
Where have you been to, my only
  one?
I've been a-wooing mother, make my
  bed soon,
For I'm sick at heart and would love
  to lie down.

What have you ate today, Billy my son?
What have you ate today, my only one?
I've ate eel pie mother, make my bed
     soon,
For I'm sick at heart and shall die
     before noon.

An older, less psychoanalytical interpretation of this rhyme is that it refers to Billy copping off* with a mermaid. Mermaids' preferred means of reproduction, for those of you not up to speed on the sex lives of water-dwelling mythical beings, is to castrate the man just at the point of climax. Then she scatters the seed on her own eggs in the way that fish do. Naturally, this would leave any man feeling "sick at heart" and maybe a little more.

Other rhymes tell of the effect that a bad marriage may have on a man:

Tommy Trot, man of law,
Sold his bed and lay on straw,
Sold the straw and slept on grass,
To buy his wife a looking glass.

Scissors and string, scissors and
     string,
When a man is single he lives like a
     king.

79

Needles and pins, needles and pins,
When a man marries his troubles
  begin.

Although there are plenty of examples in life of men running through their fortune for love, the rhyme directly above does run contrary to current research, which suggests that single men have a much glummer time of it than their married chums. So much for folk wisdom. Besides which, in the first rhyme above, who is to say that the lawyer, Mr. Trot, did not like being abused by his wife in such a manner? The most cursory of glances through the personal columns and today's newspaper headlines will reveal that legal gentlemen and other top professionals are happy to pay huge sums to be sadistically treated. So rhymes that imply that women are the downfall of men may not tell the whole story.

As noted, there is an element of bargaining in the courtship dance and a number of rhymes deal with women who try to get a better offer from their suitors, or with men trying to impress a woman by upping the stakes. In the rhyme below, the suitor is making a pitch to the divine curly locks:

Curly locks, curly locks, wilt thou be
    mine?
Thou shalt not wash dishes nor yet
    feed the swine,
But sit on a cushion and sew a fine
    seam,
And feed upon strawberries, sugar
    and cream.

While it seems that curly receives a pretty good remuneration package, the "pumpkin shell" in which "Peter, Peter, Pumpkin Eater" keeps his spouse could almost be rhyming slang for "suburban hell." Here is a man who is unable to manage his wife's aspirations until he finally succeeds in effectively stifling her by putting her in a constricting environment:

Peter, Peter, pumpkin eater,
Had a wife and couldn't keep her.
Put her in a pumpkin shell,
And there he kept her very well.

The second verse of this rhyme suggests that education might be the way to a happier coexistence, or maybe it's just that as Peter gets on in the world he can provide a better class of shell:

Peter, Peter, pumpkin eater,
Had another and didn't love her.
Peter learned to read and spell,
And then he loved her very well.

See, it's all about words and communication. But without wishing to get too grim, it is worth remembering that both women and men make mistakes for love:

There was a lady who loved a swine.
Honey, quoth she,
Pig hog, wilt thou be mine?
Hough, quoth he.

I married my wife by the light of the
    moon,
She never now gets up till noon,
And when she gets up she is slovenly
    laced,
She takes up a poker to roll out the
    paste.

Some rhymes mention tests for lovers to perform in order to sort out the posh from the wrecks. In the following, the male suitor sets his would-be lover some near-impossible tasks, only to find that she has a few implausible demands of her own:

Can you make me a cambric shirt?
Parsley, sage, rosemary and thyme.
One with no seams, or fine
  needlework?
And you shall be a true lover of
  mine.

Can you wash it in yonder well?
Parsley, sage, rosemary and thyme.
Where never sprung water, nor rain
  ever fell?
And you shall be a true lover of
  mine.

Can you dry it 'pon yonder thorn?
Parsley, sage, rosemary and thyme.
That never bore fruit since Adam was
  born?
And you shall be a true lover of
  mine.

Now you've asked me questions
  three,
Parsley, sage, rosemary and thyme.
I hope you'll answer as many for me?
And you shall be a true lover of
  mine.

Can you find me an acre of land?
Parsley, sage, rosemary and thyme.

Between the salt water and the sea
   sand.
Or never be a true lover of mine.

And can you plough it with a ram's
   horn?
Parsley, sage, rosemary and thyme.
And sow it all over with one peppercorn?
And you shall be a true lover of mine.

Can you reap it with a sickle of
   leather?
Parsley, sage, rosemary and thyme.
And bind it up with a peacock's
   feather?
And you shall be a true lover of mine.

And when you have done and
   finished your work
Parsley, sage, rosemary and thyme.
Then come to me for your cambric
   shirt,
And then you'll be a true lover of
   mine.

According to a more Freudian (and considerably fruitier) interpretation of this, the swain is really asking for the woman's virginity, with the cambric shirt representing the maidenhead, an unblemished stretch of young skin that has not been pricked. Continuing (or should that be Carrying On?) the theme, the dry well is one that no one has been down before, and he certainly wouldn't want a woman who has already borne fruit. So he's saying, "It would be good to sleep with you but I want to be the first."

She does not rule out his advances but does stress that his timing had better be spot-on*. The land revealed by low tide doubles up to mean something rarely seen, a glimpse of stocking or anything normally covered up. So she's saying, "Play your cards right . . ." but also "Are you man enough?" (the ram's horn business), "Do you fire blanks?" (the seeding), and finally she needs to know if he has a bit of élan, and is not too close with his money (the peacock feather), because she's not going to put out for just anyone.

Disaster warning?
Ladybird, Ladybird

Ladybird, ladybird,
Fly away home.
Your house is on fire,
And your children all gone.

"Ladybird, Ladybird" is a pan-European rhyme that is one of the most obviously sinister in the book, offering home destruction and the loss of one's young.

Oddly (in the context of the rhyme), ladybirds were historically often seen as a representation of good luck, and killing one was believed to bring ill fortune. They are considered a special animal to the Virgin Mary and some researchers have even traced the sacred ladybird back to the scarab beetle in ancient Egypt and linked it to the worship of Isis or her north European equivalent, Freya (also cheerfully known as Frigg), wife of Odin. Anyway, you can take it that this is a remarkable insect that carries much imagery with it.

One theory about the rhyme is that the

home and offspring represent the temples and followers of these earlier belief systems and their destruction in the face of advancing Christianity (A.D. 400). Others suggest that the ladybird leaving symbolizes the end of the old matriarchal religions that were usurped by the coming of the male sky gods, Zeus and Odin (1000 B.C.).

So you see, you can read an awful lot into a few lines once you get the hang of it. In later times of religious conflict the rhyme came to refer to the widows left after a period of persecution, Catholic widows during Protestant ascendancy and Protestant widows during Catholic. Though, broadening the theme out, it might be used to describe other forms of persecution or, as it's politely referred to, "ethnic cleansing," from the forced clearances of the Scottish Highlands to the murderous events in Bosnia. This would clearly represent a later use of a rhyme that certainly predates the Reformation. The fact that there are versions of this rhyme across the Scandinavian and German-speaking parts of Europe points to the likelihood of its being a rhyme with ancient roots.

In another link to the Continent, a popular way to get rid of a witch in central Europe was to tell her that her house was on fire. Though that does rather beg the question as to what might be an unpopular way of getting rid of a witch.

In Britain, and particularly Scotland, the ladybird is also used to divine who a person's lover might be:

> Fly over river, fly over sea,
> Fly east and fly to the west,
> Fly to the person who e'er they be,
> The one who loves me the best.

Ladybirds are not the only insects that are believed to be useful for divination. Bumblebees appearing in a room denote the coming of a visitor, whereas the sight of the first butterfly was once eagerly awaited in Gloucestershire as a means of telling one's fortune for the future year. If the first butterfly seen was white, it would mean that person would eat white bread all year. Now, in the interesting parallel universe that was Gloucestershire in the past, eating white bread meant that a person was well off. Hence people hoped to meet a white butterfly first. Today, of course, only people cooking schemey teas* involving boiling beans in run-down council blocks* prefer white bread. The well-off favour organic brown bread made from dry-stoned crushed wheat using the labour of a free-range donkey. Ironically, this is what the poor would once have eaten in rural Gloucestershire (and elsewhere). This raises a number of interesting questions. In the first place, over time will the superstition change so it is seen as good luck to see a dark butterfly? And has anyone thought to tell the butterflies of their changed position in the order of things?

Other small-animal superstitions include the belief that it was very good luck to kill the first wasp spotted in the new year, and that the dead wasp could be used as an amulet to cure illness if held under a person's chin. At least, that is according to the natural historian Pliny the Elder, who died in A.D. 79. With better scientific justification it is believed that a spider's web is good for stemming bleeding, although its effectiveness against ague and whooping cough must be questioned. Spiders themselves are generally considered lucky — or, rather, it is unlucky to kill them.

This must raise a tricky problem for the terminally superstitious of what to do when a large black spider enters their house. This is a supposed portent of death, yet, if one kills it, bad luck follows. Quite enough to put a person into a spin. Likewise killing a moth in the room of a dying person is considered a bad idea, as it is believed that this is the form in which the human soul escapes the body.

On the subject of great escapes, there is a marginally more compassionate extra verse to "Ladybird, Ladybird" that runs:

> All except one,
> And that's little Anne.
> And she has crept under
> The warming pan.

A swift tour of London?

Oranges and Lemons

Oranges and lemons,
Say the bells of St. Clement's.
You owe me five farthings,
Say the bells of St. Martin's.
When will you pay me?
Say the bells of Old Bailey.
When I grow rich,
Say the bells of Shoreditch.
When will that be?
Say the bells of Stepney.
I'm sure I don't know,
Says the great bell at Bow.

Here comes a candle to light you to bed,
Here comes a chopper
to chop off your head.
Chop, chop, chop.

At one time, this rhyme was a fair guide to parts of the City of London and its suburbs, until the eighteenth century, when "London" began its expansion from city to global metropolis.

The St. Clement's in the rhyme was near the fruit and vegetable markets of Cheapside and, more important, the dock where imported fruits once landed. St. Clement Danes on the Strand, which today peals (no pun) out the tune, is almost certainly not the one in the rhyme, as it's too far west. St. Martin's is close to where the moneylenders used to live (this is not St.-Martin-in-the-Fields near Trafalgar Square), and Old Bailey is near the site of the old debtors' court and prison at Newgate. This older court should not be confused with the current Central Courts of Justice at Old Bailey, even though the sites are very near to each other. Shoreditch was a poor area where debtors would be likely to live.

In fact, debtors from Shoreditch would go to almost any length to avoid paying their creditors. Richard Burbage, who owned the Globe theatre in Shoreditch, dismantled it piece by piece and reassembled it in Southwark, south London, to avoid payments to the landlord. After that, he didn't need to pay off too many debts, as the theatre became synonymous with William Shakespeare and made him a decent living. For the first time, Shoreditch is now becoming affluent, although the young professionals flooding the area certainly still owe huge amounts on the mortgages for their "loft-style apartments" in the old warehouses and factories.

Returning to churches, "Bow" is almost certainly St.-Mary-le-Bow, whose bells told Dick Whittington to "turn again" and within whose sound all true cockneys must be born (allegedly), and not Bromley-by-Bow, which is far too far east. Stepney, just on from Whitechapel in the East End, is famous for many things, including the meeting between the child King of England (Richard II) and the leaders of the Peasants' Revolt in 1381, who had their heads removed for general cheek, most especially for not sharing their toys with him and for treating him with insufficient respect.

Actually, that's too tenuous a link for the "chopping" part of the rhyme, although in England it was once possible to lose your head for a bewildering array of perceived misdemeanours. The last part of the rhyme is very possibly about the randomness of fortune, referring to a fate that could bring you good things (light, bed) or bad things (the chopper), no matter what your station in life and what area you were from.

Then again, there is a lesser-known version of the rhyme that opens up the possibility of something else altogether:

> Gay go up, and gay go down,
> To ring the bells of London Town.
> Bull's eyes and targets,
> Say the bells of St. Margaret's.
> Brickbats and tiles,
> Say the bells of St. Giles'.
> Oranges and lemons,
> Say the bells of St. Clement's.
> Old shoes and slippers,
> Say the bells of St. Peter's.
> A stick and two apples,
> Say the bells at Whitechapel.
> Old Father Baldpate,
> Say the slow bells at Aldgate.
> Maids in white aprons,
> Say the bells at St. Catherine's.
> Pokers and tongs,
> Say the bells of St. John's.
> Kettles and pans,
> Say the bells of St. Anne's.
> Halfpence and farthings,
> Say the bells of St. Martin's.
> When will you pay me?
> Say the bells at Old Bailey . . .

Some historians suggest that what you have here is essentially a wedding rhyme.

Old shoes and slippers were thrown at wedding couples, and there is a pleasing amount of double entendre potential, with "Old Father Baldgate" meaning phallus and "maids in white aprons" referring to the bridesmaids. As in the well-known version, the rhyme culminates with "here comes a chopper," where the sense becomes graphically clear. "Chopper" is a euphemism for penis; the "head" would be the maidenhead, traditionally lost in bed on the wedding night. As any newlyweds will vouch, the tradition continues of paying for weddings on the never-never* in order to guarantee that the memories will last a lifetime. In this way the rhyme serves as an appealing skit on courtship and marriage traditions.

The song is also used in a children's game in which two children join hands to form an arch and sing the song, while other children pass under the arch in a line. At the end of the song, which gets faster and more menacing, the two children forming the arch bring their arms down on the child passing under the arch. The child has to decide whether to be an orange or a lemon, and lines up behind one of the two parts of the arch. When all the children have been "chopped" there is a tug of war to decide whether the oranges or the lemons are the stronger.

There is a contemporary story involving citrus fruit and London that also offers a guide to the kind of neighbourhood you are in. One particular area known as St. Giles lies either side of New Oxford Street. That street was laid out in part to break up the old slum of St. Giles in the same way that Regent Street came into being partly to separate the richer folk to the west from the ne'er-do-wells of Soho. Today greengrocers and corner stores near New Oxford Street keep a particularly watchful eye on their lemons and limes, sometimes separating them from their other fruit. This is because of the large number of heroin addicts in the area who like few things better than to steal citrus fruit. This is not a belated health drive on the part of the junkies but simply due to the fact that brown heroin dissolves in citric acid, making it easier to inject.

Handbags at ten paces?

Tweedledum
and Tweedledee

Tweedledum and Tweedledee
Agreed to have a battle,
For Tweedledum said Tweedledee
Had spoiled his nice new rattle.

Just then flew down a monstrous crow,
As big as a tar barrel,
Which frightened both the heroes so,
They quite forgot their quarrel.

Despite achieving fame in *Through the Looking-Glass and What Alice Found There*, this rhyme is actually much older, predating its use by the four-eyed* cleric, Lewis Carroll, by more than one hundred years. Despite associations with the satirists Pope and Swift, the phrase "Tweedledum and Tweedledee" appears to come from an original piece by John Byrom that went:

Some say, compar'd to Bononcini,
That Mynheer Handel's but a ninny;
Others aver, that he to Handel
Is scarcely fit to hold a candle:
Strange all this Difference should be
'Twixt Tweedle-dum and Tweedle-dee!

In 1725, a bitter feud arose between the composers Handel and Bononcini. Few outsiders could see what the point of the dispute was, as there seemed very little to tell the two apart. Whoever was ultimately responsible for the final couplet, Byrom, Swift, or Pope, he had an excellent ear for assonance and alliteration that sweetens the common association of Tweedles Dum and Dee with two feuding fatties. Sadly there is no record of the composers writing a score about poets battling as to who wrote the skit in the first place.

If you would like a more contemporary example of this dispute, cast your mind back a few years to the great face-off between Blur and Oasis* in the mid-1990s. Of course, no one wrote a rhyme to commemorate this, which is a pity, because the image of Noel Gallagher and Damon Albarn being attacked by a monstrous crow is really quite pleasing.

I coulda been a pretender
William and Mary, George and Anne

William and Mary, George and Anne,
Four such children had never a man,
They put their father to flight and shame,
And called their brother
a shocking bad name.

History books do not really elaborate on what the "shocking bad name" is, but a reasonable guess might be that it begins with a "b" and nearly rhymes with "custard." The brother (or brother-in-law) referred to was called James, after his father, James II of England. James Stuart was the only one of the King's offspring to stick by his father, and later rallied the Jacobite (from the Latin for James) cause by claiming the throne as the Old Pretender. His own son, Charles (Bonnie Prince Charlie), was later known as the Young Pretender. Mary was James II's daughter and married William of Orange. Together, they ousted her father from the throne in 1689, thereby ensuring a Protestant accession.

Anne sided with her sister Mary and took over the throne herself in 1702 with her husband, George (the erstwhile Prince of Denmark). Anne was the last Stuart monarch and during her reign in 1707 the official Act of Union with Scotland was enacted (and the last legally sanctioned execution of a witch took place in 1712). The Act of Union prompted a series of rebellions in the name of James II or James the Old Pretender or a free Scotland or the Young Pretender.

Mary's marriage to William is also commemorated in the following verses, the first of which is the Scottish version and the second a more neutral comment on the marriage. A "porringer," incidentally, is a small bowl, often with a handle, for eating soup or stew.

> O what's the rhyme to porringer?
> Ken ye the rhyme to porringer?
> King James VII had a daughter,
> And gave her to an oranger.

> The second James a daughter had,
> He gave the Prince of Orange her;
> And now I think I've won the prize,
> In making a rhyme to porringer.

In the sixty years that followed the ousting of James by William and Mary, there were five rebellions attempting to restore James or his descendants to the throne. Some of these were short-lived affairs, but there were major insurrections in 1715 and 1745. In 1689, the Convention of Estates in Scotland recognized William and Mary as the rightful monarchs. The most prominent figure of this uprising was known as "Bonnie Dundee" to his friends and John Graham, Earl of Claverhouse, to everyone else. Graham was killed, despite winning a military victory at Killikrankie in July 1689, and shortly after this his armies were defeated at the battle of Dunkeld. James then raised an army in Ireland, where a local parliament had acknowledged him as King, but William defeated him at the battle of the Boyne in July 1690. James fled to France, to be joined by the last remnants of the Jacobites, the so-called "Wild Geese" (actually ten thousand Irishmen).

In 1708, in response to the Act of Union, there was a revolt that failed, and in 1715, John Erskine, Earl of Mar, raised the clans again to dispute the succession of the Hanoverians. Four years later, an army of approximately three hundred Spaniards landed at Eilean Donan Castle to no great effect. The final Jacobite rebellion kicked off when Bonnie Prince Charlie landed in Scotland in July 1745, won the battle of Prestonpans, and marched south. This is when the problems started, as neither lowland Scotland nor northern England had risen in support of the Prince and (surprise, surprise) the promised French force never materialized. They began a retreat north and the Jacobites were comprehensively routed at Culloden Moor.

Bonnie Prince Charlie fled, kilts and the use of tartan were banned, and the Highlands were systematically cleared of their people and culture over the following years. The Prince escaped with the help of Flora MacDonald, who dressed him up as her servant, Betty Burke, to get him safely to the Isle of Skye and on to France. Trannie* Prince Charlie's fortunes never recovered and he took to the bottle, moved to Rome, and died in 1788. His brother, Henry Stuart, became the last Stuart pretender, with a Jacobite court in Rome under the patronage of the Pope until 1807, hatching ever madder and more far-flung plots. They became like the exiled Russian nobility in 1920s America and, while it's unlikely that any of them ever drove taxis for a living, they became a progressively sadder bunch, staggering up to passers-by, saying, "I coulda been a pretender." Other symbols of Jacobitism were coopted by manufacturers of shortbread biscuits* as handy images to put on their tins. In this way the Jacobites, as Alexei Sayle* noted, have joined the Garibaldis and the Bourbons in the great pantheon of rebels who inspired the marketing of biscuits.

Georgy Porgy

Georgy Porgy pudding and pie,
Kissed the girls and made them cry.
When the boys came out to play,
Georgy Porgy ran away.

One popular theory is that this is a satire on the Prince Regent (1762–1830). George was a vain man despite being described, with some accuracy, as "a fat, half-German yob with a brain the size of a pea" in the TV series *Blackadder*.* He later became George IV, and his life has some interesting parallels with today's monarchy. Among these are the facts that he waited decades to inherit the throne and ignored his wife while carrying on with an already married older woman who was widely lambasted in the media. Better yet, he liked to meddle in current affairs and write letters to ministers, particularly on the matter of architecture. It's possible he had a point, as some of that Georgian stuff was pretty racy and some right carbuncles were placed in front of beautiful Stuart buildings.

The link to George is plausible, as the rhyme was not known before the nineteenth century, a fact that probably squashes the more popular notion that it is about George Villiers, the Duke of Buckingham (1592–1628), son of George Villiers (a minor nobleman) and father of George Villiers, the second Duke of Buckingham. Just to make it clear who is who, George Villiers became a regular at the royal court in 1614, and in 1615 he was appointed to the position of Gentleman of the Bedchamber for James I, where he prospered greatly under the King, going on to become an earl in 1617 and a marquess in 1618.

In case you hadn't guessed it yet, the popular conjecture is that the King and George Villiers were lovers. The King even made a proclamation of their love before the Privy Council, saying, "You may be sure that I love the Earl of Buckingham more than anyone else . . . I wish to speak on my own behalf and not to have it thought to be a defect." James also allegedly had the Henry VII Chapel in Westminster Abbey remodelled to include adjacent tombs for himself and Villiers so that even death would not separate them.

So the business in the rhyme about kissing the girls and making them cry is supposedly about George mucking up the King's relationships with various women. While this is unproven, he did manage to ruin the planned marriage of James's son (later Charles I) to the Infanta Maria in Spain. One of the repercussions of this was a call from the Spanish ambassador for Villiers to be executed for his conduct while he was in Madrid. James took no notice and Villiers himself gained some popularity by calling for war with Spain on his return, though his popularity was short-lived after he was blamed for the failure of a later military expedition. Despite this, when Charles became king, Villiers was the only major personage from the court of James to maintain his position and, when Parliament attempted to impeach him for yet another failed campaign, Charles had the House of Commons dissolved before it could put him on trial. Villiers survived until 23 August 1628, when he was stabbed to death near where Lambeth Bridge currently stands. His ghost is said to haunt the area, and every year at 5 a.m. on 23 August people gather on the bridge in the hope of witnessing a repeat of his murder. It's worth mentioning too the entirely unrelated coincidence that one of London's most famous and long-established gay nightclubs, Heaven, is on Villiers Street near Charing Cross.

So that's all good speculation about gay royals and stupid royals, but it's now time to rein in the conjecture, as the earliest written version has no mention of anyone called George at all and instead goes like this:

Rowley Powley, pudding and pie,
Kissed the girls and made them cry;
When the girls begin to cry,
Rowley Powley runs away.

Making the obvious assumption that Rowley Powley is a corruption of roly-poly (a fat, round child, one stuffed with pudding and pie), what we have is an incredibly modern rhyme about the dangers of being a tubby child. The rhyme is saying that lard-arses won't get anywhere with the birds and might be bullied. This has interesting echoes in some of the current government (and other) propaganda aimed at adolescents who overeat and take too little exercise.

Once again, it seems that the British genius for song puts the case much more succinctly than could any number of health advisory leaflets or annoying adverts for gymnasiums currently doing the rounds. It is worth pointing out that, in 2003, 14 per cent of fifteen-year-olds and 8 per cent of six-year-olds were defined as obese, and that thirty-one thousand people die of obesity-related diseases every year in the UK. Among the proposals suggested by the Department of Education to improve this situation is one to distribute free fruit to children. Surely this cannot be the same Department of Education that a generation ago allowed schools to sell off playing fields to help them become more business-focused and competitive? Or the society that allows poor payments to teachers and the threat of lawsuits (in relation to Outward Bound* courses) to cut back on out-of-school activities? Or the one that, through its drive to compete via league tables*, causes ever-portlier kids to get driven in cars to ever-farther-away schools? Still, it's nice to get a bit of fruit since they took the milk away.

Maybe there is another solution if we return to the "kissing girls" bit, however. Aldous Huxley makes fine use of the rhyme in the novel *Brave New World*, although he does alter the sense somewhat in the following version:

> Orgy-porgy, Ford and fun,
> Kiss the girls and make them one.
> Boys at one with girls at peace;
> Orgy-porgy gives release.

Now, leaving aside the invocation of the god Ford*, because we now live in post-industrial times (that is part of the problem as well, too many sedentary jobs), the gist of the original rhyme is that fat boys scare away girls. However, sex is a good way of burning off calories, so maybe that is the solution (for teenagers anyway), or would be if the government weren't equally consumed by fears of teenage pregnancies and sexually transmitted diseases. So all things considered, it is unlikely that anyone will be recommending that particular energetic pastime as a means of solving obesity. Besides which, if the old rhyme is correct, who will kiss the fatties in the first place?

A few stops beyond Barking?*

As I Was Walking o'er Little Moorfields

As I was walking o'er little Moorfields,
I saw St. Paul's a-running on wheels,
With a fee, fo, fum.
Then for further frolics I'll go to France,
While Jack shall sing
and his wife shall dance,
With a fee, fo, fum.

There are a number of extra verses to this rhyme depicting a whole series of improbable happenings, such as "killing a man when he was dead." This verse was printed up and named "The Lover's Harmony," but evidence suggests an earlier song, again containing a series of nonsensical or barmy* events. So-called "mad songs" were apparently very fashionable in the eighteenth century and fed nicely into the craze for nonsense verse for children that followed in the nineteenth. What makes this particular bit of mad verse stand out is the reference to Moorfields, because Old Bethlem (Bethlehem) Hospital, better known as Bedlam, London's most infamous asylum, was moved to Moorfields in 1675 from its original site next to Liverpool Street station.

The first Bedlam building, at Bishopsgate, belonged to the Priory of St. Mary Spital. It was confiscated by King Edward III and subsequently turned into an asylum. The Old Bedlam was unable to cope with the growing madness of London, and pressure grew for it to move to larger premises away from the City. This may sound strange, as it moved to Moorfields, which is today at the heart of London. Even in the eighteenth century, however, it was still considered to be at the edge, and in the thirteenth century Bishopsgate had been at the city's borders. In a strange contemporary twist, the two sites are just south of the newly fashionable Old Street/Hoxton area, full as it is of insane fashion, experimental clubs, strange medications, and people exhibiting the kind of behaviour that might once have got them incarcerated in the hospital.

Robert Hooke was appointed City Surveyor, and designed the "new" Bethlehem Hospital at the Moorfields site. Above the door were sculptures commissioned from the Dutch artist Caius Gabriel Cibber, one representing mania, or raving madness, the other, melancholy insanity. The building was developed with some care to resemble the Tuileries Palace, home of the French King. This was a nice touch, implying a link between the deranged of England and French royalty. There was a fashion for visiting the bewildered, which brought together all classes of London society. The response of the visitors (ranging from cackling laughter to tormenting the afflicted) caused some commentators to suggest that the wrong crowd was being locked up. Prostitutes loitered in the area to pick up trade from those excited by what they had seen, and the whole area had a circus feel about it. Peter Ackroyd, in his marvellous biography of London, takes up a theme of eighteenth-century writers who saw Bedlam as a metaphor for the City at the time — overcrowded, rushed, full of frenetic energy, a London in microcosm — and before we look down at the entertainment value of visits to a psychiatric hospital, it would be good to consider the scenes outside the Big Brother House and other popular TV reality shows. In all honesty, is there really much difference in our enjoyment of the condition of the tortured and locked up?

Not everyone at the time was happy with the situation, though, and there was a sense among a minority of Londoners that there was something indecent about the whole business. Thomas Tryon was less complacent and complained in 1695 that "It is a very undecent, inhuman thing to make a show by exposing them, and naked too, to the idle curiosity of every vain boy, petulant wench, or drunken companion."

Admission was one penny, and the annual visitors raised 166 pounds, 13 shillings, and 4 pence (old money) a year for the hospital. Unfortunately, unlike similarly confined human participants in TV reality shows, the inmates did not get a cut of the takings, even though their antics were what drew people to the hospital and provided the inspiration for artists, novelists, and songwriters. The earliest-known song referencing Bedlam is "Tom O' Bedlam," which was presented at the royal court in 1618. "Maid in Bedlam" (below) dates from the eighteenth century:

Abroad I was walking,
One morning in the spring.
I heard a maid in Bedlam,

So sweetly she did sing.
Her chains she rattled in her hands,
And always so sang she.

In 1807, Bedlam moved over the water
to the site now occupied by the Imperial
War Museum, and what better comment
could there be on the madness of war? As
London expanded, the final resting place
of Bedlam, like many other institutions for
the unwanted, moved to the green belt
around London, the orbital of the M25*
near Beckenham. Since the 1980s, when
many of the great asylums were closed and
their inhabitants released into the gentle
care of the community, many former asylums have been turned into luxury housing
developments. You could argue that one
would have to be slightly barmy to buy a
flat in a former asylum in the M25 corridor*. Either way, Bedlam still functions
as a hospital despite the close attentions of
the West Beckenham Residents' Association, who are quite obsessed about having
such a facility near them. Peculiar that they
failed to spot the hospital when they
bought their houses, as it's been there
since 1930.

If you want to see lunacy in London
today, you don't have to pay a thing. It is

sufficient to loiter in just about any reasonably populated area for long enough. There is something roaring and bonkers about the city that no freshly minted theories about urban stress can fully explain away. Perhaps those of us who live here should just celebrate the psychosis. After all, there is an organization called Mad Pride which arranges events around the city to just that end. Of course, those of you who don't live here simply assume we are all cracked to put up with London life anyway, and regularly come along for a glimpse at the asylum. Though you generally have the good taste to pretend that what you are really doing is popping down for a bit of shopping or to see a musical (as if anybody would *really* travel from, let's say, Barnsley* just to see *Grease*). No, the real point of walking across Moorfields, or anywhere else in London, is surely just to note the fruitiness of its inhabitants.

By 'eck, pet!

Elsie Marley
Is Grown So Fine

Elsie Marley is grown so fine,
She won't get up to serve her swine,
But lies in bed till eight or nine,
And surely she does take her time.

And do you ken Elsie Marley, honey?
The wife that sells the barley honey?
She lost her pocket and all her money,
Aback o' the bush in the garden, honey.

Elsie Marley wore a straw hat,
But now she's got a velvet cap,
She may thank the Lambton lads for that,
Do you ken Elsie Marley, honey?

Elsie keeps rum, gin and ale,
In her house below the dale,
Where every tradesman up and down,
Does call to spend his half a crown.

Several rhymes celebrate well-known good-time girls, but Elsie's story is better chronicled than most. The four verses above are part of a lengthier song printed in the 1750s but already popular, telling the story of Elsie (or Alice) Marley, the innkeeper of the Swan in the village of Picktree in northeast England, who was born in about 1715. Little is known of her background other than what is stated above, or of her husband, except that his name was Ralph. This was also the name of her grandson, who left a detailed record of her adult life as related to him by his father, Elsie's son, Harrison Marley. In his account, the only quibble he has with the life of Elsie as portrayed in the verse is the notion that she was lazy. According to her grandson, she was most active at all times and a very astute manager of the business. He specifically explains the verse about her losing her pocket and all her money: that happened on a trip to Newcastle, where she was due to pay a brewer's bill of twenty guineas[*]. She was jostled in a crowd and someone stole the cash she was carrying.

Elsie was a celebrated local character with a wide circle of friends and many male admirers, and the implication in the verses included here is that it was not just the quality of her ale that attracted men to her establishment. The first verse sometimes says "feed the" rather than "serve her" swine, in which case the suggestion is that she is above menial tasks like feeding pigs and is perhaps getting above her station. However, while "serve her" and "feed the" could potentially mean the same thing, the use of "serve her swine" might also be taken as a slur on her customers. There is even a faint echo from the tale of Odysseus and his return from the Trojan wars, when the crew lands on the island of Aeaea and is transformed by the sorceress Circe into pigs.

Perhaps that's pushing her reputation as a seductive beauty too far, but who knows? According to a writer on the *Newcastle Magazine*, she was a tall, refined-looking, slender woman. The remaining verses (not included above) run through all the different types of men (sailors, farmers, gentlemen, and others) who are drawn to Elsie and spend their money at her establishment. The Lambton lads in the third verse were apparently five brothers who shared Elsie's affections. So here we have a woman keeping a family together, which is very charitable indeed. What her husband thought of all this is not recorded, though he survived her and remarried after her death in 1768. Her death was not quite as colourful as her life but was fairly dramatic. She went out of the house on the morning of 5 August with a high fever and in her delirium fell into an old coal-pit full of water and drowned. Quite a damp ending for such a fiery character.

Elsie's fame was established early on in her life, and the song was a popular dance favourite long after her death. By 1745, when the last Jacobite rebellion took place, the song (including the bit about her losing her money) was already well enough known for Dutch mercenaries travelling north to fight Bonnie Prince Charlie to sing the following song, based on the original:

Saw you Eppie Marley, honey,
The woman that sells the barley,
honey?
She lost her pocket and all her
money,
Following Jacobite Charlie, honey.

They are also alleged to have used the sign at the Swan for target practice. This seems most unlikely behaviour from soldiers of a country associated with tolerance of women of easy virtue, unless they really did think Elsie Marley was a Jacobite. There is no evidence of Jacobite sympathies anywhere, but it might just have been a handy song to remind others of what can happen if you fall in with the wrong crowd, and as Elsie Marley had become such an iconic figure by then, she was as good a person as any to hang the song around.

Yankee Doodle

Yankee Doodle came to town,
Riding on a pony.
He stuck a feather in his cap,
And called it macaroni.

The earliest reference to this rhyme is 1768, when a Boston periodical, *Journal of the Times*, mentions it as a top tune of the era. Allowing for journalistic ineptitude in picking up dance-hall trends, of course, it must be assumed that the rhyme was in existence some time before then, although the belief that it was composed by a Dr. Shuckburgh in 1758 appears to be erroneous.

The song was initially popular among British forces during the War of Independence, as a mocking appraisal of the American soldiers' inability to fight (and indeed dress themselves) properly. After the battle at Bunker's Hill, the US troops themselves adopted it as a favourite marching song and threw it back at the Brits, to the annoyance of one British officer, who said, "It ['Yankee Doodle'] is now their paean, a favourite of favourites . . . a lover's spell, the nurse's lullaby." They even played it when the British army came down to sign the surrender documents. So here's early proof that Americans have a decent sense of comic timing and irony, whatever some commentators might say.

There is always something pleasing, of course, about turning someone's song against them, and certainly London football supporters revelled for years in a re-working of the Liverpool anthem "You'll Never Walk Alone." The altered version is as follows and, barring a 1980s revival, is very out of date, as the economy is now fairly bright in the future European City of Culture:

> Sign on, sign on,
> With hope in your heart,
> 'Cause you'll never get a job,
> You'll never get a job.

They used to follow this by waving fist-fuls of fivers*.

The "Yankee Tootle" or "Yankee Doodle" was originally an English take on American folk music, composed to be played on the flute or whistle. The words, which were added later, were really secondary to the tune and were ad-libbed in the manner of a rapper, just to keep the dance hall jumping. If you can't see it as a dance-hall tune, try setting the following version from 1775 to a reggae rhythm and reading it out loud in a Jamaican accent:

> Yankee Doodle keep it up,
> Yankee Doodle Dandy,
> Mind the music and the step,
> And with the girls be handy.

After the US gained its independence in 1776, many supplementary verses extolling the virtues of the US soldiers were added, while in Britain, satirical equivalents directed against Americans were in circulation. There were literally dozens of different versions, as this simple melody was fitted to different themes. To give some idea of how many, a play written in 1787 called *The Contrast* contains a line about "Yankee Doodle" in which one character says that he knows only one hundred eighty verses but that "our Tabitha at home knows the lot."

Even the four best-known lines are subject to alternative wordings ("speckled pony" and "Kentish pony," for example), but the core story remains the same: man rides into town on pony, man sticks feather somewhere, man calls it an Italian dish. Whatever its origins as a song, the word "Yankee" has become a nickname for all things American (or more specifically New England). That he rides a pony rather than a horse might suggest relative poverty, and sticking a feather in his cap is certainly an attempt to put on airs. Of course, he could be riding a pony just because "horse" doesn't rhyme with "macaroni," but that rather begs the question of why it would need to rhyme with macaroni.

To answer that, you need to know what macaroni is. Of course macaroni is an Italian dish and very tasty indeed. But it was also the name given to themselves by a bunch of fashionable youths who appeared in London in 1770. These ultra-dandified young men were at their peak in 1772 and 1773. Previous youth movements had been known as Beaus and Fribbles (no, really), and obviously two hundred years later there were the New Romantics to keep the tailors in business. The Macaronis knew that, to quote Adam Ant, "ridicule was nothing to be scared of." They were chiefly young men of noble birth who, after taking the Grand Tour of Europe, returned to Britain with fresh ideas about clothes and food, much in the way folk today return from the Far East with tribal tattoos and new philosophies. Erstwhile Prime Minister Horace Walpole blamed the phenomenon on Clive of India*. He reasoned that without the East India Company making so much money and without all that money flooding into London, a movement such as the Macaronis could not possibly have existed.

The Macaronis sported huge wigs supported by natural hair bunched on the shoulders, ornate tight jackets that hugged the figure, and trousers to match. They also favoured huge nosegays in their buttonholes. Like the Mods and Punks much later, they took London by storm and had an influence way beyond their original numbers, to the point where even clergymen started combing their wigs and subtly altering their clothes to more closely resemble the Macaroni style. Amusingly in an age of industrial booze swilling, the Macaronis' drug of choice was tea and capillaire (a syrup prepared with maidenhair fern). Oh, and of course a certain type of pasta, which they tried to include at every mealtime.

The phrase "feathers in their caps" (meaning something significant achieved) was first used in the eighteenth century, but the custom of wearing a feather as a badge of honour goes way back and across many cultures. Native Americans added feathers to their headdresses to denote animals or men killed, or victories achieved. More recently, hunters in Scotland and Wales would pluck feathers from the first bird killed in the hunting season and place them in their caps.

The most popular surviving lyric is essentially a putdown by the fashionable cosmopolitan British of some hayseed colonial who thought he was quite the dandy and that, by sticking a feather in his hat, he could emulate the trendy peacock youth of London town. This sort of thing happens all the time, of course. Bored suburban teenagers think they are quite ghetto when they don the supposed apparel of the inner city, while others should remember that a few piercings and creative use of eyeliner do not a Marilyn Manson make.

What's good about "Yankee Doodle" is that it is an early example of Britain and the United States taking the same dance tune and remixing it back and forth between them. Throughout history this has continued. The United States comes up with blues. The British take the style and, hey presto, you have the Beatles and Rolling Stones. US soul music and, later, house find a ready audience in Britain, where they are reinterpreted and sent back, reinterpreted again and returned to Britain. And so on and so on, back and forth, a dance of nations in some ways oddly in tune with each other, which has to be a good thing.

London's Burning

London's burning, London's burning,
Fetch the engines, fetch the engines,
Fire! Fire! Fire! Fire!
Pour on water, pour on water.

As early as the first century A.D., London had precautions against fire in the form of *vigiles,* or "bucket boys." By medieval times, each ward was responsible for the fires in its area and, as late as 1657, James Howell* claimed that there was no place better armed against the fury of fire. Less than a decade later, on 2 September 1666 (at least, that was the day that diarist Samuel Pepys was woken at 3 a.m. to be told about it), a fire started in Pudding Lane near the Thames. It burned for five days and left over 70 per cent of the city in cinders. It had been a hot August, and the thatch and timber of the closely built houses, together with a strong south-westerly wind, produced conditions ideal for the spread of fire. It was not just the houses of the poor that burned; St. Paul's Cathedral, a larger structure than today's church, disappeared, and the lead from its roof ran molten through the streets. Perhaps oddly, the official death toll stood at only six by the time the fire was stopped near Fetter Lane on the edge of the legal district. This prompted the wry comment that perhaps God is a lawyer. Either that, or he feared the ensuing litigation if the Inns of Court* around contemporary Holborn were allowed to burn.

A combination of a change in wind direction, which made the fire turn back on itself, and the belated pulling down of houses to create fire breaks, eventually brought the blaze under control. The orders to pull down houses came from King Charles II and were very much against the wishes of the householders. Seeing an opportunity to prove that a king could be the leader of his people (in the aftermath of the Civil War), Charles had decided to take direct control. He may also have been concerned by the thought of the fire spreading to Westminster and his own residences. Samuel Pepys, who credits himself with advising the King on this policy, also took an active role in the house clearances, and it is from his diaries and those of John

Evelyn* that many of the best accounts of the fire come.

All the usual suspects — Jews, Masons, Catholics, witches, and, of course, the French — were blamed. This was a bit unfair, particularly on the French, as they invented one of the simplest ways to extinguish fire, the *couvre feu* (a metal cover to go over the open hearth), which later developed into the English word "curfew." A Frenchman, Robert Hubert, was hanged in October 1666 for allegedly throwing fire bombs into houses on Pudding Lane, even though it was later found out he was not even in the country at the time. Forensic investigations using twentieth-century methods and reconstructions point to an accidental start to the fire in the ovens of the baker Thomas Farriner. He lived in Pudding Lane, where the monument to the Great Fire is today, east of London Bridge on the north bank.

Perhaps more interesting than the search for blame is the case of Solomon Eagle, who is credited with having predicted London's destruction by plague and fire in the years leading up to the Great Plague of 1665 and the fire of the following year. To emphasize his prophecy, he walked the streets with a bowl of fire balanced on his

130

head and announced all the usual things that the enthusiastically religious tend to (that people should return to God and mend their ways or London would face a Sodom and Gomorrah-style destruction).

Fire and London are old acquaintances, and the scorched soil below the surface details previous conflagrations. London had burned in A.D. 60 courtesy of Boudicca and her Iceni warriors and again over a dozen times in the following twelve centuries. Later, there was the great fire on Tooley Street in 1861 and the Blitz of the 1940s. Boudicca has a statue commemorating her exploits near Westminster Bridge. Though her body is said to lie under platform 9 of London's King's Cross station, just another East Anglian commuter who passed away waiting for the train to Cambridge. The statue of another fire-starter, Commander "Bomber" Harris, stands in the grounds of St. Clement's Danes on Fleet Street. He was responsible for the thousand plane raids and the resulting firestorms that destroyed Hamburg, Dresden, and Leipzig in the 1940s.

The first attacks of the Blitz were on the suburbs, but on 7 September 1940 wide swathes of east London around the docks were hit. Over the following nights the bombers moved west so that, by the full moon on 15 October, many thought that their city was indeed going to face destruction on a par with that of 1666. As in 1666, the soil was exposed in areas of the city that had been built on for centuries, resulting in an explosion of flower growth and other wildlife. Some, like the poet Stephen Spender, took comfort from the fact that the immensity of London meant that it was simply too imposing to be destroyed. Across the city, folk took up Churchill's slogan "Business as usual" and affected a bloody-minded nonchalance.

"London's Burning" might have been appropriate for the Blitz but, while it clearly predates it, the rhyme does not go back as far as the Great Fire. A closer association with the origin of the rhyme can be made with the nineteenth-century great fire on Tooley Street. Tooley Street runs a block in from the Thames, from London Bridge east towards Tower Bridge. This area was formerly the larder of London, with foodstuffs imported through the local docks and processed in the streets behind them. Today, it is home to the offices of the Mayor of London and a Foster* of prestigious office developments.

The Tooley Street fire broke out on Saturday, 22 June 1861. It started in a jute warehouse at Cotton's Wharf, which was completely destroyed. The warehouse soon collapsed and fell onto a nearby building that contained highly flammable products such as tallow, tar, and resin. These exploded, projecting flaming materials far and wide that set fire to other warehouses and buildings before spreading to an American steamer, four sailing boats, and many barges on the Thames. The fire burned fiercely through the night, was visible for fifty miles, and, despite being under control by the second day, was reported to have smouldered in the ruins for more than six months.

One of the people to die in the Tooley Street blaze was Firemaster James Braidwood, who had been brought in from Edinburgh to set up the London Fire Brigade. Braidwood was succeeded by Captain Massey Shaw, who issued his firemen with a new-style helmet made of brass and was responsible for many improvements in equipment, such as steam fire engines and street alarms. Under the Metropolitan Fire Brigades Act of 1865, the fire protection of London was handed over to the Metropolitan Board of Works, and the Metropolitan Fire Brigade, the forerunner of the present

London Fire Brigade, was born.

Whatever its origins, the rhyme certainly serves to remind the population of London that fire is an ever-present danger. Its theme was taken up more recently by the band the Clash, fronted by Joe Strummer. Their song "London's Burning" was a scathing indictment of the dullness of mid-1970s London, when the city was burning with boredom and seething with tensions. One of the last public performances by Joe Strummer, whose death in December 2002 was a great shock to his many admirers, was, fittingly, a benefit concert for striking firemen.

A quiet word about lullabies

Baby Love,
My Baby Love

Rock a bye, baby, in the treetop,
When the wind blows the cradle will rock,
When the bough breaks the cradle will fall,
And down will come baby, cradle and all.

Despite being one of the best-known nursery rhymes/lullabies in the world, its origin is unclear. Perhaps because of this, there are a pleasing number of theories as to what it means (if anything). These range from its being a reference to the baby Moses in the bulrushes to a warning about hubris. A more popular interpretation is that this simple lullaby originated in America at the time of the Pilgrim Fathers. This story goes that the new settlers saw mothers from the Wampanoag tribe make a cradle from birch bark and suspend it from a tree. The wind would rock the cradle and lull the child to sleep, with the obvious danger that the wind might be so strong that it would cause the cradle to fall from the tree. A windier theory is that the verse is English in origin, that the baby in question is the son of King James II, and that an ominous wind brought William of Orange to claim the throne and cause the fall of the House of Stuart. This might appear to fit until history rather annoyingly gets in the way. William of Orange married into the Stuart line and his sister-in-law Anne (a Stuart) inherited the throne. Besides which, how many nursery rhymes can one person be involved in? Greedy, I would call it. There is also a Scottish version which runs:

I placed my cradle on yon holly top
O hush a ba, baby
O bah lilly loo.

However, it doesn't take too much lateral thinking to realize that the rhyme could be a simple description of a family tree, as Marina Warner suggests. The "baby" is simply the youngest branch, which will eventually become older and break as its predecessors did. The "baby" moves down the tree as fresh branches (succeeding generations) grow above, and the wind is simply an allegory for time passing. This might fit with the notion of lulling a child to sleep, secure in its position as part of the overall structure of the family.

The word "lullaby" comes from the obsolete English word "lulla," possibly based on a Greek word to describe the sound of lapping water. The understood meaning is a soothing refrain, specifically a song to quieten children or charm them to sleep. In other songs the child might be promised something good, such as the rabbit skin in "Bye, Baby Bunting." It would appear, though, that lullabies are not always meant to make a baby feel secure. In fact, there is a decent case to be made that their primary intention is to scare the youngster, homeopathically as it were, by alluding to something frightening. These rhymes forewarn the baby, who is able to build up an immunity to the nightmares ahead, whether these are phantoms in the form of ogres, unlikely threats in the form of wolves, or the very real possibility of accident, as in the following from *Tom Thumb's Pretty Songbook* (1744):

Piss a bed, piss a bed,
Barney Butt.
Your bum's so heavy,
That you can't get up.

137

Then again, it could be that lullabies just express the frustration and anger of a parent who has been driven to distraction by the child's wailing and resorts to threats.

Baby, baby, naughty baby,
Hush, you squalling thing, I say.
Peace this moment, peace, or maybe,
Bonaparte will pass this way.

Baby, baby, he's a giant,
Tall and black as Rouen steeple,
And he breakfasts, dines, rely on't,
Every day on naughty people.

Baby, baby, if he hears you,
As he gallops past the house,
Limb from limb at once he'll tear you,
Just as a pussy tears a mouse.

And he'll beat you, beat you, beat you,
And he'll beat you all to pap,
And he'll eat you, eat you, eat you,
Every morsel, snap snap snap.

Mothercare* would no doubt frown upon this sort of thing, but it serves as a good reminder that cruelty to children is hardly a new thing, and that the threat of corporal punishment (and worse) has always hung over the nursery.

One of the interesting things about the rhyme above is that it was clearly composed for children. The most popular version refers to Bonaparte (Napoleon), so it can be dated to the early nineteenth century. Bonaparte can be replaced by a host of folk devils, however, with versions citing Oliver Cromwell ("as tall as Lincoln's steeple"), Menshikov (a Russian commander in the Crimean War), and even members of the Nazi hierarchy. The reference to Cromwell might push the rhyme's origin way back into the seventeenth century; obviously, any reference to the Nazis brings it into the twentieth. The psychology is clear, with the threat of an external bogeyman beyond parental control invoked to silence a noisy child. In the film *The Usual Suspects* the idea is mooted of a super villain, Keyser Soze, who clearly scares the criminals but in turn becomes a spook story that they pass on to their children: "Rat on your pop and Keyser Soze will get you."

Before cinema gave us an unending diet of exotic spooks (a real globalization of terror?), such bugaboos would be more likely to be national or even regional figures of fear. There was also an early attempt at political indoctrination at the cradle in some households. European anti-Semitism is full of stories about gentile children being sacrificed and, in some traditions, it is the Jew (or gypsy) who fulfils the Bonaparte role. In communist and other nineteenth- and twentieth-century political traditions, the figure of the factory owner might crop up, while in earlier rhymes religion rather than politics might provide a parent with the figure of fear to pass their prejudices on to a future generation. King Herod, slaughterer of the innocents, was a character well suited to the role.

Many lullabies and children's stories feature child-eating cannibals. They also express a prejudice against outsiders, a convention that seems to be reawakened every summer in the UK with one terrible incident of abduction or murder after another heightening fear among parents and children. What grabs far fewer headlines is the grim fact, which all available statistics in the UK bear out, that children actually face far greater threat from their own parents and other relatives. Despite contemporary panics about Internet chat rooms, in the UK many more children are still killed by those close to them than by strangers. A tradition that has, of course, found its way into song.

There was a lady dwelt in York,
Fal the dal the di do.
She fell in love with her father's clerk,
Down by the green wood side.

She laid her hand against a stone,
Fal the dal the di do.
And there she made most bitter moan,
Down by the green wood side.

She took a knife both long and sharp,
Fal the dal the di do.
And stabbed her babes unto the heart,
Down by the green wood side.

As she was walking home one day,
Fal the dal the di do.
She met those babes all dressed in
    white,
Down by the green wood side.

She said, "Dear children, can you tell,"
Fal the dal the di do.
"Where shall I go? To heaven or
    hell?"
Down by the green wood side.

141

"O yes! dear mother, we can tell,"
Fal the dal the di do.
"For it's we to heaven and you to hell."
Down by the green wood side.

Paved with gold?

Turn Again, Whittington

Turn again, Whittington,
  thou worthy citizen,
Turn again, Whittington,
Lord Mayor of London.

Make your fortune; find a good wife,
  You will know happiness
    all through your life.

Turn again, Whittington,
  thou worthy citizen,
Turn again, Whittington,
thrice Mayor of London.

Richard (Dick) Whittington was born in 1357 and achieved a great many things in his life, yet now he is best known for having a pet cat and, unlike Mrs. Thatcher, turning*.

Dick was the younger son of the Lord of the Manor of Pauntley in Gloucestershire.

When his father died, the oldest son inherited the estate, leaving Dick homeless. He travelled to London, where he served an apprenticeship as a mercer (trader in cloth), worked his way up and became the main supplier of fine cloths to King Richard II and, later, King Henry IV. From this, he became very rich and often lent large sums of money to the crown. In return, he was allowed to export wool without paying customs duty on it, which made him even richer. Dick became a City alderman, or magistrate, in 1393, and Lord Mayor of London in 1397. He was re-elected the following year, and again in 1406–07 and 1419–20. So that's four times, not three as the song claims, although he was elected only three times — the first time, he was appointed by King Richard. Whittington died in March 1423 with no children, and his will dictated that his great wealth be used to the benefit of the City, as presumably his beloved cat had passed on already. The money was used to establish an almshouse, a college of priests, and a library, and to carry out a number of other public works. These included improvements to the water supply and the building of a public lavatory, which became known as "Whittington's longhouse."

So, all in all, a thoroughly good sort. But what about the cat? The earliest references to this appear in a comedy, published in 1605, about London life called *Eastward Ho!* in which a character refers to "the famous fable of Whittington and his pusse." Whittington was also the subject of a ballad printed in the same year. No one actually knows if he ever had a cat, although it's a pleasing idea and sounds a good deal more practical than the newts a more recent London Mayor (Ken Livingstone) has for pets. *Harlequin Whittington*, the first recorded pantomime with Dick Whittington as its subject, was performed in 1814, and the legend continued to be embellished in the following decades, helped by the introduction of new characters like King Rat (believed to be a reference to the Black Death).

One part of the Dick Whittington story, his return to London, is worth explaining in greater detail. He hears the bells at the top of Highgate Hill calling him back to the city. In the past, London's church bells defined the city in a way that current residents cannot imagine, with our huge volume of background noise. Foreign visitors would remark on the duration and volume of the parish bells that pealed out across the city. It would be quite likely, for example, that the Great Bell at Bow could be heard all over London from Lambeth in the west to Rotherhithe in the south-east. Nowadays, of course, folk in Lambeth can barely hear Big Ben just across the water at Westminster and, over in Rotherhithe and Bermondsey, the clattering construction of loft-style riverside apartments shatters the peace even if Millwall FC* happens to be playing away.

Contemporary London dwellers have other sounds to confirm their existence, and these have more to do with money than with the spiritual calling of church bells. They range from the trains, traffic, and planes that deliver people and goods in and out to the cacophony of the costermongers* and the jabber of the terminally busy into their mobiles*. Having said that, London was always a hubbub of commerce and trading. Whittington's Mercers' Company is a good example, as it was incorporated by Royal Charter as early as 1394 and is the premier livery company of the City of London. The order of precedence was decided by the Lord Mayor of London in 1515, following years of dispute between merchant tailors and skinners as to who went sixth and who went seventh, hence the phrase "being at sixes and sevens." Livery companies, or guilds, began in medieval times as a means of protecting the interests of particular trades, and today there are one hundred three City livery companies, some of whom are fairly modern (Environmental Cleaners, for example) while others (like the Loriners, who make stirrups and other harnesses for horses) have a longer pedigree. Some trades, such as international bankers and tax advisers, have no livery at all, and thus, presumably, no class.

Dick, however, belonged to one of the trades with plenty of prestige. It seems a pity to have to unpick the idea that Whittington started life as a poor man and found gold on the streets of London, with or without the aid of an intelligent feline, as there are relatively few examples in the UK (of men anyway) of the sort of log-cabin-to-White-House stories that the US exalts in. He wasn't born into poverty but nevertheless he did achieve great fame and fortune (what greater fame than having a panto* named after you?). Through the centuries, the notion of London's streets being (metaphorically) paved with gold has continued to be such a lure that people are continually astonished to find that they are not.

In Whittington's time, Westminster and the City of London had separate governments, with the Mayor of London heading up the City of London, based at Guildhall. In the City of London, the Lord Mayor ranks immediately after the sovereign and acts as the capital's host in Guildhall and Mansion House. Nowadays a person can be Lord Mayor only once. At the end of the twentieth century, a new post of Mayor of London was created to govern London in general rather than the square mile of the City of London. This is an elected role, voted for by all citizens, and brings with it powers to direct policy and major initiatives to benefit the people of Greater London.

Dick Whittington is one of London's most famous characters and, in a reverse of the process that sees tourists turning up at Baker Street looking for the "real" Sherlock Holmes, is wrongly believed by many to be fictional. One address that you might think would be associated with Whittington is Turn Again Lane near the Holborn viaduct. Sadly, the road's name has a much more pedestrian provenance: It was once an alley that stopped at the water's edge at the River Fleet, where there was no bridge, meaning that you had to turn again in order to get anywhere. More interesting, the remains of a mummified cat were found in the tower of St. Michael Paternoster Royal, the church in which Dick Whittington was buried in the fifteenth century. The church was rebuilt in 1694 by Sir Christopher Wren after the Great Fire, however, and the cat sacrifice actually dates from then.

Ding Dong Bell

Ding dong bell,
Pussy's in the well.
Who put her in?
Little Johnny Green.
Who pulled her out?
Little Tommy Stout.
What a naughty boy was that,
To try to drown poor pussy cat,
Who never did him any harm,
And killed the mice in his father's barn.

"Ding Dong Bell" was first printed in *Musicks Miscellanie* in 1609, although a similar verse (Jacke boy/Ho boy newes/The cat is in the well/Let us ring now for her knell/Ding dong ding dong bell) has been traced to 1580. The theme of bells tolling in reference to death appears in several of Shakespeare's works, including *The Taming of the Shrew*, *The Merchant of Venice*, and *The Tempest.* In later versions, the rhyme was changed to a tale about a cat that runs out of milk and a kind boy who puts more cream into pussy's saucer, this neutered, and frankly unbelievable, version ending:

What a kindly boy was that,
To help a poor pussy cat,
Who never did any harm,
But played with the mice in his father's
  barn.

In 1949 Geoffrey Hall wrote a book, *New Nursery Rhymes for Old*, that toned down a number of rhymes, including this one. In Hall's version, pussy is *at* the well and *plays* with the mice in the barn. However, certain morally concerned individuals had already expressed criticism of this particular one in the nineteenth century, as they believed that the lyrics encouraged children to throw cats into ponds.

So, ignoring the bowdlerized version, what we have is a rhyme about children's cruelty to cats. The debate around this rhyme is akin to that in the modern age about violent video games, films, and music: are they encouraging young people to misbehave or merely reflecting behaviour that already occurs? It's peculiar that some people should be so cruel to cats, as, historically, they seem to be held in pretty high esteem by humans, Mr. Whittington's puss being a prime example. Charles Booth, researching in the nineteenth century, quotes an elderly resident of the East End who said that there had been widespread cruelty to cats in the past but in his lifetime this had changed to a more compassionate attitude. He even cited an elderly streetwalker who distributed meat to strays, a sort of prototype cat woman. So throughout the nineteenth century, possibly as a result of laws enacted against animal cruelty (1822) and the activities of the RSPCA (Royal Society for the Prevention of Cruelty to Animals, set up in 1824), cruelty to cats, and animals in general, became, if not less common, certainly less socially acceptable. Though sadly, the habit of drowning unwanted kittens still persists.

It could be considered odd that Johnny Green didn't show greater respect to an animal that carries more symbolism and superstition than any other creature. They were worshipped as gods in the Middle East, feared as witches' familiars in Europe, and credited with powers of prophecy in China. The Egyptians, no doubt, really loved their cats, and during excavations in the ruins of Tell Basta in

1887 a graveyard with thousands of mummified holy mousers was discovered. Many were sent to Britain, where a few ended up in museums, whilst the rest were sold off as fertilizer. Sadly, none arrived in time to enter the first official cat show in the UK, at Crystal Palace in 1871. London's most famous cat, apart from maybe Mr. Whittington's, is Chaucer, the Customs-House cat, named after the writer of *The Canterbury Tales*, who once held a top post in the customs office. Cats were very useful for keeping rats away from the wharves where the imports came in, and every Customs-House cat is called Chaucer. Entertainingly, every September, when Customs House opens its doors to the public, a civil servant dresses up as a giant tabby to greet visitors.

The musical *Cats*, based on T. S. Eliot's *Old Possum's Book of Practical Cats*, also celebrates the antics of our furry friends. However, without wishing to disillusion anyone, these are just people dressed up. In 1758, there was the real thing. A man called Bisset trained his pussies to dance and even play a few notes on musical instruments. Their performances sold out at London's Haymarket Theatre and Bisset made his fortune. Later, a Mr. Capeli, who exhibited his felines at Bartholomew Fair, took up the idea. His cats were far more practically minded, grinding knives, roasting coffee, and, aptly, in view of the rhyme, ringing bells.

Here We Go Round the Mulberry Bush

Here we go round the mulberry bush,
The mulberry bush, the mulberry bush,
Here we go round the mulberry bush,
On a cold and frosty morning.

This is the way we wash our hands,
Wash our hands, wash our hands,
This is the way we wash our hands,
On a cold and frosty morning.

This is the way we wash our clothes,
Wash our clothes, wash our clothes,
This is the way we wash our clothes,
On a cold and frosty morning.

The rhyme has been added to over the years rather in the manner of "Simple Simon"; any activity can be included, forming the basis of a game for young children. The song itself is a nice, simple rhyme charting a few everyday activities taking place on a chilly morning. Nothing sinister here, surely? Mulberry bushes are an attractive enough shrub, and it was common in years past to hang clothes on bushes to dry, so the scent of the tree or bush would freshen up the clothes. That might explain the reference to washing clothes, but the key to understanding the rhyme has to be the title and whether the phrase "round the mulberry bush" actually meant anything. Other bushes have symbolic meaning after all: for example, in pre-industrial Britain a male suitor would leave a sprig of holly outside the house of his intended, whereas a sprig of gorse (the "smelly bush") would be deposited outside the house of, shall we say, easier girls.

According to legend, the mulberry fruit was originally white and became crimson from the blood of Pyramus and Thisbe. The tale is that Thisbe was to meet her lover at the white mulberry tree inside a cemetery in a suburb of Babylon. She was surprised by a lion and cut herself but managed to flee. As she did so, she dropped her bloodied veil. Pyramus, thinking that the lion had devoured his beloved, promptly slew himself, and when Thisbe found him, she took her own life. The blood of the lovers stained the white fruit of the mulberry tree into its present colour. In other cultures, folk apparently used to dance around mulberry bushes on midsummer night in order to ward off evil. As if these tales were not dark enough, there is a bleak origin to the phrase "here we go round the mulberry bush." Mulberry trees were planted in prison yards and "go round and round the mulberry bush" was quite literally what the prisoners did every day to get their exercise. Furthermore, the phrase "been round the mulberry bush" became a euphemism to describe someone who had been locked up in prison.

Mulberry bushes are not as common as they once were in Britain. In the late seventeenth century there was an attempt to cultivate a domestic silk-weaving industry inspired by the success of French Huguenot weavers. Mulberry plantations were set up across London, including one on the site currently occupied by Buckingham Palace's gardens. There are reminders of these plantations all over the city in street names such as Mulberry Place, Road, Crescent, and eight Mulberry Closes. Further evidence of a silk industry can be found in Tenter Grounds in EC1*, situated between Petticoat Lane and Fashion

Street. Silk yarns were dried, or "tentered," in the open air, and tenter grounds were where dyed silks were stretched between posts using hooks — this is where the phrase "being on tenterhooks" comes from. By the mid-eighteenth century, twenty-two hundred master weavers employed more than thirty thousand workers in London.

In order to protect the London silk-weaving industry, the government banned all imports of silken materials. Britain did well as a silk-weaving nation but, sadly, the plan to actually produce the silk there failed. Returning to the mulberry plantation on the site of the gardens of Buckingham Palace, this was known as a gay cruising area, so it's quite pleasing to note that there is some continuity of use by today's gay valets. When Buck House gardens became walled off, the main cruising area shifted into nearby Hyde Park, while prostitutes operated out of St. James's Park.

It should hardly come as a surprise that London's parks have always been used for sexual purposes. It is perhaps more shocking that this rhyme and the mulberry bush should be associated with suicide, sex, and gaol*.

A proper paddy?

This Old Man

This old man, he played one,
He played knick-knack with his thumb,
With a knick-knack, paddy whack,
Give the dog a bone,
This old man came rolling home.

This old man, he played two,
He played knick-knack with my shoe,
With a knick-knack, paddy whack,
Give the dog a bone,
This old man came rolling home.

This old man, he played three,
He played knick-knack on my knee,
With a knick-knack, paddy whack,
Give the dog a bone,
This old man came rolling home.

The verses continue from four to twelve
with:

He played knick-knack at my door.
He played knick-knack on his hive.
He played knick-knack with his sticks.

He played knick-knack with his pen.
He played knick-knack on my gate.
He played knick-knack, rise and shine.
He played knick-knack in my den.
He played knick-knack up in heaven.
He played knick-knack, dig and delve.

This is a lovely nonsense verse dating from the nineteenth century which helps children to learn how to count. Although, in view of the various contemporary concerns involving old men, perhaps the lines about the knee and visiting the den might be worth reconsidering.

The words in the repeated part of the rhyme all have meanings but seem strung together just for their sounds rather than to make sense. "Knick-knack" dates back to 1673 to describe a trifling bit of furniture or keepsake, with a later word, "knick-knackery," used to describe any form of pleasing artifice or larking about. Nowadays the word "charm," or perhaps "chicanery," would be nearer the mark. "Rolling home" is most associated with drunkenness and "give the dog a bone" might be a handy way of keeping the dog quiet or could be a euphemism for something else. The term "paddy whack" is interesting, as its first meaning (1881) was an Irishman but by 1889 it had come to mean a rage or a passion, as in "she went into a right paddywhack when we took her toys away." Put together, there is the attractive idea of a slightly duplicitous old Irishman rolling home drunk and covering his tracks by silencing the dog and playing a range of silly games. So there is meaning to be found if only you look hard enough!

The phrase "getting in a right paddy" sort of lives on, with its connotations of pointless rage (brought on by drink or not) and, of course, "Paddy" is still used as a term for an Irishman. The linkage of the terms sits rather well with English fears at the time, both of the Irish (this was the period of the Fenian terrorists and Home Rule debates) and about law and order in general. As a term, "paddy whack" fits nicely, being an unwarranted rage associated with the fiery temperament of the Irish, very alien and un-English. Perhaps one reason why paddy whack is not such a popular term these days is that another has eclipsed it. That word is "hooligan," which first appeared in England at around the same time. In the summer of 1898, police reports and later newspaper articles started mentioning a gang of young street toughs who called themselves "the hooligans." These too were given (erroneous, in all probability) Irish connections.

Whether the rhyme has any other meaning is unclear. However, the gist of the following chilling greeting to Liverpool's Lime Street station in the 1980s by a bunch of scallies* was absolutely crystal to anyone hearing it: "Mick! Mack! Paddy! Wack! Let's get a woollyback!"

This cheerful sub-ballad (accompanied by a series of sheep noises, if memory serves) was a call to arms by the largely Irish Liverpudlians (Mick and Paddy) and their mates (wacks and macks) against those from outside the city. "Wack" is a Scouse term for "friend" or "pal," most likely deriving from an old army word for rations, containing in it the implication of sharing the rations and therefore of camaraderie. "Mack" would represent the Scottish part of the city's racial make-up. Curiously, the verse makes no mention of the long-standing black community or one of the oldest Chinese communities in the UK. A more accurate description of what is, after all, one of Britain's oldest multicultural cities should go: "Mick, Mack, Chinese, and black . . ." etc. Even "Scouse" (and the attendant dish) comes from the north European sailors' food, lobskaus*, which was brought to Liverpool by foreign mariners. "Woollyback" is a term that refers to folk from sheep-rearing places like Yorkshire and Wales but less specifically to anyone not from Liverpool, including the Wirral, as well as places like Warrington, Widnes, and Wigan. Is there any connection to the original rhyme here? No. But it does place the verse into a context approaching the original meaning of "paddy whack," and I still have the scars to prove it.

Penny for them?

Remember, Remember

Remember, remember
the fifth of November,
Gunpowder, treason and plot.
There is no reason why
gunpowder and treason,
Should ever be forgot.

Guy Fawkes, Guy Fawkes, 'twas his intent,
To blow up the King and the Parliament.
Three score barrels of powder below,
Poor old England to overthrow.

By God's providence he was catch'd
With a dark lantern and lighted match
Holler Boys, holler boys,
make the bells ring,
Holler boys, holler boys,
God save the King.

"Remember, Remember" is a bit of a seasonal one, referring to the attention-grabbing events that took place on 5 November 1605. The rhyme is still quite well known, and bonfires are still lit and fireworks exploded on that day. It is perhaps a shame that some traditions, such as urchins dressed in their mothers' cast-off clothes collecting money for a bundle of rags and the eating of seasonal foods like parkin*, are less observed these days.

There is a peculiar duality in our approach to Guy Fawkes and Bonfire Night in general. Ostensibly, we are celebrating his demise by burning his effigy on bonfires, yet there is an element of celebrating the attempt to blow up Parliament mixed in there as well. There is nothing specifically anti-Catholic about the contemporary event, Lewes bonfire and a few others aside, although its roots lie (as do those of so many songs) in the struggles between Catholics and Protestants in the hundreds of years after the Church of England was established.

The story starts in Lambeth at the home of John Wright, where three gentlemen met in secret to discuss their troubles. King James VI of Scotland had only recently taken on the English throne as James I but, despite promises of a relaxation in the anti-Catholic laws, it now appeared that the new King would be even more severe towards Catholics than his predecessor had been. Robert Catesby and his cousin Thomas Wintour discussed with Wright a plan to blow up the King and the House of Lords at the next Opening of Parliament. In May 1604, Thomas Wintour enlisted the help of a Yorkshire mercenary named Guy Fawkes, who had distinguished himself on the Continent in the Spanish army. Others joined in, including Robert Wintour, Christopher Wright, Thomas Percy, John Grant, Ambrose Rokewood, Robert Keyes, Sir Everard Digby, Francis Tresham, and Catesby's servant, Thomas Bates.

In March 1605, Thomas Percy was able to use his connections at the royal court to rent a cellar right under the House of Lords, and Fawkes filled the underground storehouse with thirty-six barrels of gunpowder hidden beneath coal and wooden sticks. However, ten days before the Opening of Parliament, Lord Monteagle, a Catholic lord, received a letter warning him (and some friends) to avoid Parliament for the opening on 5 November. Monteagle immediately showed the letter to Robert Cecil, the Secretary of State. Cecil had the vaults beneath the Lords searched on 4 November and, when the gunpowder was discovered, Guy Fawkes (standing around whistling and playing with matches) was overpowered. The other conspirators fled, although they were eventually captured and never made their rendezvous on Parliament Hill, where they planned to watch the fireworks down in Westminster. There are conspiracy theories that the Earl of Salisbury had actually instigated the plot in order to frighten the King into recognizing the Catholic threat and that Guy Fawkes was an agent provocateur.

Oddly, Parliament Hill is still a popular spot from which to watch fireworks, as it is one of the highest points in north London. Primrose Hill, west of Camden, which hosts one of London's better firework displays, was more of a mound than a hill in Fawkes's time. It was built up in the nineteenth century when rubble from the expanding railway and canal networks was deposited to create the hill we know today. Parliament Hill was formerly known as Traitors' Hill, and there is some debate as to whether it got its name from the 5 November conspirators. It was renamed during the English Civil War, when the Parliamentarian forces set up a gun emplacement on it. In an odd switch, Parliament Hill is thought to have been a site of religious ceremonies. However, the Druid religion reorganized itself in more recent times and by the late twentieth century was celebrating its observances of the longest and shortest days on the "new" Primrose Hill.

Very recently indeed (November 2003) scientists calculated quite how much devastation would have occurred had the Catholic weapon of mass destruction gone off in 1605. Dr. Geraint Thomas, who rejoices under the title of Head of Explosion Studies at the University of Wales, used the weight of explosive to work out how it would have affected its surroundings. The five thousand pounds of gunpowder could have caused chaos and damage over a five-thousand-foot radius, enough to destroy Westminster Hall and the Abbey, with streets as far as Whitehall being affected.

If this calculation is correct, the explosion would certainly have taken out the MI5 headquarters near the north end of Lambeth Bridge, had it been there at the time. MI5 is the security service charged with protecting the UK from terrorist threats today. Having developed considerable expertise against the IRA* in the past decades, it now turns its attention to threats from Al Qaeda. Both, like Guy, claim to represent religious minorities. Among the more colourful sections of MI5 is a unit devoted to what can be described only as unobtrusive security measures; a good example of their work can be seen outside their own headquarters. In many parts of London, old cannons are filled and used as decorative street bollards*, so there is nothing strange about the ones outside Thames House. Except that they are not decorative but rather a clever attempt to deflect anyone entertaining the notion of driving a vehicle (packed with explosives or not) into the building. Other people in that department toil on far more recherché schemes, the most Pythonesque perhaps being the notion of defence shrubbery. This is foliage that repels by use of thorns and/or scent.

It is odd that certain sections of the British public can celebrate an attempt to blow up the King and his ministers in the past, yet, in contemporary Britain, the whole notion of explosions and public safety initiates a completely different debate, involving the lack of rubbish bins at tube stations, widespread use of CCTV,* and restrictions on the sale of fertilizer. In all probability, the idea of burning a representative icon at the death of the autumn (and 5 November is very close to the official end of British Summer Time*) harks back to older folk festivals to mark the end or beginning of the year. The Samhain* festival marks one of the two great doorways of the Celtic year, Beltane* on 1 May and Samhain in November. A number of other cultures also burn effigies at key points in the calendar. In Normandy, for example, a squalid effigy, scantily clad in rags and a battered old hat, is destroyed on Ash Wednesday. In this case, he is a representation of evil and dissipation that is being exorcized from the community, although no one seems to stand around collecting euros for the Guy in this case. That might be the key to our ambivalence when it comes to Guy Fawkes — the burning of the effigy takes us back to older, pre-Christian events that have been celebrated in these islands for thousands of years.

Animals in Nursery Rhymes

In the United States, nursery rhymes are frequently referred to as Mother Goose rhymes, after the earliest collections published there. The term is less popular in Britain, possibly because "goose" once meant prostitute over here, but more probably because "Mother Goose" covers both nursery rhymes and fairy stories in the United States and the two are treated separately in the UK. The phrase has been traced to a 1650 book, *La Muse Historique*, in which the line *"comme un conte de la Mère Oye"* ("like a Mother Goose story") appeared. In 1697, Charles Perrault used the term in a published collection of eight fairy tales, which included "The Sleeping Beauty," "Little Red Riding Hood," and "Cinderella." It would appear, then, that Mother Goose has French origins. Presumably when word of this gets out stateside, she'll be renamed, just as sauerkraut became "freedom cabbage" in the First World

War, and French fries became "freedom fries" in more recent times. The single most important promoter of Mother Goose as a writer of children's rhymes was John Newbery, in a volume published in 1766. There is apparently an earlier book, published in 1719 in Boston, but no one alive has ever seen a copy. So it gets worse; not only was Mother Goose French, but the first English-speaking "Mother Goose" was a bloke.

Despite the above information, Mother Goose is usually portrayed as a kindly elderly lady, and this association with gentility has helped to disassociate some of the rhymes from their more raucous origins, particularly in the United States. For example, it's rare for the second verse to be included in one of the more popular American lullabies:

Hush-a-bye, baby, don't you cry, go
   to sleep, you little baby,
When you wake you shall have all the
   pretty horses,
Blacks and bays, dapple and grays,
   coach and six little horses.

Hush-a-bye, baby, don't you cry, go
   to sleep, you little baby,

Way down yonder in the meadow lies
  poor little lambie,
The bees and the butterflies pecking
  out his eyes,
The poor little thing cries Mammie.

What's that about? Is it a verse of
promise (go to sleep and you'll get . . .)
followed by threat (don't go to sleep and
you'll get . . .)? Or is a comparison being
made between the fortunate position of the
human child with the sweet lamb, the
bleating of the lamb sounding like the cry
of a child?
There is a strong literary tradition of
using animals to expose the idiosyncrasies
of humans, often in order to make a hu-
morous point. Sometimes they are used to
make an analogy with human behaviour or
to expose human vanities ("Old Mother
Hubbard"), at other times the animals are
just the butt of cruelty ("Ding Dong
Bell"). Greek mythology is full of anthro-
pomorphic beings, with Zeus turning up as
a swan or a bull and all those centaurs and
satyrs. Monastic scribes of the Middle
Ages frequently used animal imagery to il-
luminate their texts. It was often safer to
use animals as a metaphor in political
satire rather than risk being accused of

treason. There is a theory that sections of Izaak Walton's *The Compleat Angler,* published in 1653, aside from being one of the finest books ever written on fishing, is also a critique by Walton, as a Royalist, of the leadership of Oliver Cromwell and his Parliamentarians. Oliver's army is represented in the book as otters, the enemies of the fisherman.

There have been several attempts to classify animals by their traits and relationships with mankind. George Orwell drew on this tradition in writing *Animal Farm* in his use, for example, of the horse to represent the nobility of labour. Many nursery rhymes originate in a period that covers a shift in British culture from one where cruelty to animals was the norm to one of mawkish sentimentality. Bear- and bull-baiting, for example, were once hugely popular, and the English were widely regarded as one of the cruellest people in Europe when it came to animals. However, by the mid-Victorian period, they could perhaps already be regarded as the softest. In this context, it is worth remembering that the RSPCA was famously set up (1824 and becoming Royal in 1840) long before the NSPCC (National Society for the Prevention of Cruelty to Children,

1889 and no royal patronage). Something that Philip Mundella, sponsor of the Prevention of Cruelty to, and Protection of, Children Act 1889 alluded to when he said he was "anxious that we should give children almost the same protection that we give . . . domestic animals."

There are a number of theories explaining the changing attitude towards animals, not least the massive urbanization of the nineteenth century that removed the bulk of the population from contact with (farm) animals on a daily basis. The reforming zeal of the nineteenth century had an effect as well, with its attempts to morally instruct and improve the manners of the lower orders. In some cases this meant rewriting songs, in others writing verse from the point of view of the animal. The novel *Black Beauty* is the classic example here. The theory is that, once an animal has been imbued with human characteristics, it is harder to treat it inhumanely. A swift glance at the sales of bacon after the movie *Babe* was released confirms this theory (at least in the short term).

Cruelty to animals came to be seen as socially unacceptable, and the notion of the family pet (as opposed to a working cat, say) grew among the middle classes.

Behaving in a civil fashion to animals became a symbol of civilization or, rather, a symbol of being middle class. Dog licences were brought in, and the Kennel Club was set up as dogs became domesticated, though the following rhyme does seem to confuse the actual role of the dog within the home:

A girl in the army,
She longed for a baby,
She took her father's greyhound,
And laid it in the cradle.
Lullaby, Baby bow wow wow,
Long legs hast thou,
And if it wasn't for thy cold snout,
I would kiss thee now.

Nursery rhymes are just one manifestation of the confused status of animals in British society. There is a pet cemetery in Hyde Park and a war memorial in Kilburn, north-west London, for all the animals that died in the Great War. The division between what might be seen as an underclass attachment to working/fighting animals and the middle-class sentimentality towards the family pet still bubbles to the surface in such passing panics as the Dangerous Dogs Act of the 1990s. Throw in the arguments about fox hunting, often seen as class-based, and it hardly seems surprising that folk songs should reflect this ambivalence. However, the story that perhaps best exhibits the contradictory feelings towards animals in the UK is known as the Brown Dog Affair and centres on attitudes towards vivisection.

In 1906, Battersea Council* decided to erect a statue of an unknown dog in order to show its support for the anti-vivisection cause. The statue was set on top of a water fountain in the Latchmere Estate, not far from the river, and was supposed to represent all those animals that had died in medical experiments. But this outraged sections of the medical community and a bunch of medical students marched on Battersea, intent on smashing the statue. People from Battersea responded by gathering together to defend the dog, less out of any entrenched views about vivisection and more because there was a bunch of students behaving leerily on their estate (*plus ça change,* one might say). The battles between the two sides got so bad that the statue ended up with a police guard.

The fights over the statue brought to a head a simmering debate about vivisection that culminated in a substantial demon-

177

stration by pro-vivisectionists in Trafalgar Square, some of them carrying dead dogs on poles. They didn't march unopposed; thousands of "brown dog supporters" (caninistas?) turned up as well. The result was a series of running battles, in fact the largest brawl in central London until the poll tax riots of 1989. For several years, there was an uneasy truce on the brown-dog front until a Conservative council was elected in Battersea and removed the poor mutt from his plinth, casting him into the Thames. In a retaliatory gesture against all things Tory, the Greater London Council in the 1980s unveiled a new statue of a brown dog in Battersea Park to honour his lost ancestor.

These antics disappointingly have nothing to do with the following rhyme:

Oh where, oh where has my little dog
    gone?
Oh where, oh where can he be?
With his ears cut short and his tail
    cut long,
Oh where, oh where can he be?

This is actually a children's version of a comic verse written by Septimus Winner in 1864 called "Der Deitcher's Dog," which portrays a hound that comes to a sticky end, and takes a sideswipe at German food. The original rhyme continues:

I loves mine lager 'tish very goot beer,
Oh where, Oh where can he be?
But mit no money I cannot drink here,
Oh where, Oh where ish he?

Across the ocean in Garmanie,
Oh where, Oh where can he be?
Der deitcher's dog ish der best
    companie
Oh where, Oh where ish he?

Un sasage ish goot, bolonie of course,
Oh where, Oh where can he be?
Dey makes em mit dog und dey
    makes em mit horse,
I guess dey makes em mit he . . .

Moving on to swine, pigs in wigs or otherwise make numerous appearances in nursery rhymes and children's literature, even though there is a great deal of guilt in the human relationship with hogs and they are frequently associated with unattractive human traits. In the following rhyme one pig is a burglar, another greedy, another hypochondriac, another a snitch, and the last physically too weak to fulfil his greedy ambitions.

This pig got in the barn,
This pig ate all the corn,
This pig said he wasn't well,
This pig said he'd go and tell,
And this pig said — weke weke weke
Can't get over the barn door sill.

The argument runs that we despise pigs because, despite the fact that we rear them amidst filth, they are still close to mankind, kept in a sty near the house rather than in a faraway field. In order to make our behaviour acceptable, the pig is demonized as a dirty animal, even in the Christian tradition, and seen as lacking the redeeming characteristic of personality that might be attributed to another animal, such as the dog (whether brown or otherwise). This is a theme that is pleasingly picked up in the film *Pulp Fiction* in a conversation between two hired hit men that runs roughly like this:

"So according to that argument, if a pig had a better personality, he'd cease to be a dirty animal?"
"We'd have to be talkin' 'bout one charmin' pig. It'd have to be the Cary Grant of pigs."

Another odd characteristic of the pig in rhymes and other literature is its association with male mannerisms and men in general. Many more animals used in rhymes are female. "Goose" and "hen" are still used affectionately to describe women in some parts of Britain, whereas "bitch" and "cow" are negative yet widely used terms of abuse. In rhymes, if the gender of a species is specified it is more likely to be female, and often used to express double meaning. So, to return to Mother Goose, in the following rhyme is this a real goose or a motherly woman?

Cackle, cackle, Mother Goose. Have
   you any feathers loose?
Truly I have, my pretty fellow, half
   enough to fill a pillow,
Here are quills, take one or two, and
   down to make a bed for you.

If that one is equivocal, the next rhyme leaves little room for confusion by clearly linking the hen to such "wifely" duties as housekeeping:

I had a little hen, the prettiest ever seen,
She washed up all the dishes and
   kept the house clean.

Where have all the sparrows gone?

Who Killed
Cock Robin?

Who killed Cock Robin?
I, said the sparrow,
With my bow and arrow,
I killed Cock Robin.

Who saw him die?
I, said the fly, With my little eye,
I saw him die.

Who caught his blood?
I, said the fish, In my little dish,
I caught his blood.

Who'll make the shroud?
I, said the beetle,
With my thread and needle,
I'll make the shroud.

Who'll dig his grave?
I, said the owl,
With my pick and shovel,
I'll dig his grave.

Who'll be the parson?
I, said the rook, With my little book,
I'll be the parson.

Who'll be the clerk?
I, said the lark, If it's not in the dark,
I'll be the clerk.

Who'll carry the link?
I, said the linnet, I'll fetch it in a minute,
I'll carry the link.

Who'll be chief mourner?
I, said the dove, I mourn for my love,
I'll be chief mourner.

Who'll carry the coffin?
I, said the kite,
If it's not through the night,
I'll carry the coffin.

Who'll bear the pall?
We, said the wren,
Both the cock and the hen,
We'll bear the pall.

Who'll sing a psalm?
I, said the thrush,
As she sat on a bush,
I'll sing the psalm.

Who'll toll the bell?
I, said the bull, Because I can pull,
I'll toll the bell.

All the birds of the air fell
a sighing and a sobbing,
When they heard the bell toll
for poor Cock Robin.

One rather obvious interpretation is that this rhyme might relate to an early case of habitat destruction, with the cocky sparrow better suited to the developing urban climate than the more rustic robin. More in the spirit of this book are two theories that offer remarkable explanations for the rhyme. One is that it relates to the downfall of the man regarded as Britain's first true Prime Minister, and certainly the first to reside at 10 Downing Street, Robert Walpole. The second is that the rhyme tells a much older story and relates to the demise of the Norse god of hair loss, Baldur. Also, before anyone gets carried away with the notion of bulls flying in the penultimate verse and dismisses what follows as a flight of mad-cow-inspired nonsense, "bull" is a truncation of bullfinch.

Support for the Walpole theory comes

from the rhyme being about a well-loved figure who is killed in public and mourned by everyone, and yet there is no implied punishment of the murderer. The verses describe Cock Robin's death and the various roles all the birds will play in the funeral. The idea is that once Walpole was out of power, everyone (even his enemies) could pay tribute to him and say what a great fellow he was. This sort of hypocrisy is an ongoing feature of public life today. The fact that Walpole left office in 1742 and the first-known publication of the verse was in 1744 also makes him a good contender.

Sir Robert Walpole (1676–1745) was a key political player for decades. Despite being impeached for corruption in 1701, he became Chancellor in 1722 after cunningly handling the investment fiasco known as the South Sea Bubble. He was extremely popular with both the King (George I) and the British public for his key policies of war avoidance, nonintervention in European politics, solid financial practice, and liberalization of trade. George I had every reason to like Walpole, as he was part of a coterie of Whig politicians who helped George and the Hanoverian line take the throne in the face of a strong challenge from the son of James II. On a more personal level, Walpole kept the King sweet by giving his mistresses pensions and titles. He also allowed Edmund Gibson, Bishop of London, to handle Church matters and took steps to keep dissenters happy, so he had the religious pressure groups on his side. Just as in US elections today, it's often the religious and women (the so-called "soccer moms") who are needed to swing the vote.

Anyway, from 1722 to 1742 Walpole was the leading politician, stumbling only in 1739, when Britain became involved in a war with Spain. George II was in favour of the war and became Britain's last king to lead his troops into battle. Walpole, who thought the war was unnecessary, did not provide the dynamic leadership needed during wartime and, when the war went badly, the Tory opposition accused him of not supplying enough money for the British armed forces. Walpole gradually lost the support of the House of Commons, and he was forced to resign from office in February 1742. So, here is a man whom everyone knows, ostensibly respects, and mourns, yet somehow has his political career killed off.

The second theory relates to the Norse

myth of the death of Baldur, whose real role in the Norse pantheon was as the god of truth and light. He was the son of Odin and Frigg (stop sniggering at the back), and his knowledge of healing herbs and runes made him a favourite among the people. Now, unlike gods in other pantheons, the Norse gods suffered the misfortune of not being immortal, which seems to put them in division two as far as divinities go. So when Baldur started having nightmares about his own demise, it was taken very seriously. The other gods catalogued everything that might possibly cause Baldur harm, from diseases to creatures and weapons. With the list in hand, Baldur's mother, Frigg, set out to exact assurances from these entities that they would not harm Baldur. When she had completed her mission, Frigg returned to Gladsheim, the gods' meeting hall, for a celebration. After a few rounds of drinks, the gods decided to test Baldur's invulnerability by throwing things at him, ranging from small pebbles to war axes. Late in the day, Loki, who is essentially the Norse god of taking the piss*, turned up and asked why people were throwing weapons at Baldur. Frigg explained about the promises she'd exacted. Loki kept asking her questions until she finally revealed that there was one thing she hadn't askcd because she thought it too small and inconsequential: mistletoe. Loki set off to the forest to get himself a branch, then returned to the festivities at Gladsheim and sought out Baldur's blind brother, Hodur, god of darkness, who was in a corner because he couldn't aim and therefore couldn't participate in the test of Baldur's invulnerability. Loki told Hodur he would help him take aim and handed Hodur a piece of mistletoe. Hodur was grateful and accepted the offer, and then he chucked the branch straight into Baldur's chest, killing him instantly. So again, a well-loved figure is killed off in public, or at least in front of his friends.

The notion that the verse predates Walpole is supported by the rhyming of owl with shovcl, which in Old English would have worked, whereas obviously to the modern ear it jars. The rhyme would have worked that way up to the Elizabethan era, when the word changed from "showl" to the more modern "shovel." Another hint that the rhyme was known before the eighteenth century (whether to do with Baldur or not) is the depiction in a fifteenth-century stained-glass window at Buckland

Rectory, Gloucester, of a robin pierced through the heart with an arrow. Allusions to the killing of a robin in a story written in 1508 and German versions of the same tale suggest a pre-Walpole origin too. However, as with several other rhymes, this does not mean that the verse was not re-worked and republished as a skit on the fall of the Walpole ministry, as it was a century later by Byron in a savaging of the media over the death of John Keats:

> Who killed John Keats?
> I, said the quarterly,
> So savage and Tartarly,
> 'Twas one of my feats.

Over the past century, it was the supposed murderer of Cock Robin — the sparrow — that many more people became concerned about. Just what has happened to all the sparrows in Britain's cities? Though the following rhyme might offer a clue, it's probably wrong, as boys rarely play with bows and arrows these days, being too busy with heavier ordnance:

> A little cock sparrow sat on a green tree,
> And chirruped and chirruped, so merry
>   was he,

A naughty boy came with his wee
    bow and arrow,
Say he, "I will shoot this little cock
    sparrow."

The "cockney sparrer," or house sparrow, is a social creature whose interests include a fondness for dust baths and feasting on insects. The cockney sobriquet came about in the nineteenth century, when the gregarious little creature was an often-seen fixture of London's parks, gardens, and squares. Its first decline in numbers came between the wars, as horse transportation became less popular — the sparrow had enjoyed feeding on grain spilt from nosebags or undigested in dung. The recent fall in numbers has been much steeper, with a 59 per cent drop in house sparrows in London between 1994 and 2000 alone and a further 25 per cent drop the following year. So, who did kill Cock Sparrer?

Cats and other predators are obvious culprits, and chemicals in "environmentally friendly" lead-free fuel a less apparent one. Chemicals in the fuel do not dispatch the sparrows directly, but they do kill the insects that sparrows feed on, as do garden pesticides. Another hypothesis is that the fashion for decking and generally tidier gardens has reduced the sparrow's habitat, and modern architecture tends to be less accommodating to nesting birds. In rural areas, the blame for the sparrow's decline is clearer. Herbicides and pesticides encourage weed-free crops, destroying wild flowers and thereby reducing the availability of insects. Increasingly efficient farming methods mean there is less spilt grain after harvesting and no stubble is left, and harvesting itself occurs earlier in the year, leaving no food in August for juvenile sparrows at the end of the breeding season. So, who killed Cock Sparrer? We all did, though maybe it's what he deserves for killing Mr. Redbreast.

Little Boy Blue

Little boy blue,
Come blow your horn.
The sheep's in the meadow,
The cow's in the corn.
But where is the boy
Who looks after the sheep?
Under the haystack,
Fast asleep.
Will you wake him?
No, not I,
For if I do
He's sure to cry.

"Little Boy Blue" could be used to describe any situation where leaders are failing in their duty. For this reason it has been associated with Cardinal Wolsey, who, under Henry VIII, let all manner of chaos loose in the religious affairs of England. As the son of a butcher, he probably had a literal as well as figurative take on animal husbandry. But there is little else of substance to back up this theory.

There are possibly stronger associations with Charles II during the time of his exile in Europe. The rhyme was a criticism of his whiling away time, leading the good life in Paris, drinking fine wine, and perhaps (as he also spent a good deal of time in the Netherlands) doing nice things to his head with herbs. All of this convivial living was for some reason represented as sleeping "under the haystack."

While he was away indulging himself, Charles was ignoring the dreadful state of affairs in his own country, where sheep in the meadow and cows in the corn are metaphors for extreme disorder among his subjects. The rhyme is a lament by the remaining Royalists that the country was in disarray, lacking a king to lead it (no Leviathan figure, for those familiar with Hobbes's philosophy). Even these Cavaliers, however, are critical of Charles, as the final lines contain a suggestion that he might lack a certain moral fibre and should be more vigorous in reclaiming the throne.

Viewed objectively, Charles had good reason to sleep under the haystack and have a nice time of it. Many people would have been reluctant to return to a country whose leaders had removed their father's head and promised the same for them if they could only be caught. When Charles did eventually return, with the Restoration, he did not forget his dad. It could even be said that he quite lost his own head in his desire for revenge. Unfortunately for him, the people directly responsible for his father's death were dead themselves, but Charles wasn't the sort of man to let a trifling detail like that worry him. He had Cromwell, Bradshaw, and Trenton, three of the main Parliamentarians, dug up. He then had their corpses tried and the heads put on spikes. Needless to say, none of the three had much to say in their defence. Allegedly, their ghosts can now be seen in conference with each other, gliding across Red Lion Square in central London, where the corpses were kept before their trial and second "death." Perhaps not a bad place for them to be, as Red Lion Square, with the Conway Hall at its north-east corner, even today has associations with debaters and revolutionaries.

The notion of the ghosts chattering is true to their behaviour in life, for, when not organizing revolutions, forming New Model Armies, and decapitating monarchs, the Parliamentarians liked nothing better than a good discussion. Tolerance of dissenting arguments was not universal, though, as the revolutionary Levellers found to their cost after the famous Putney Debates. The Levellers wanted voting rights for all adult males, annual elections, complete religious freedom, an end to the censorship of books and newspapers, the abolition of the monarchy and the House of Lords, trial by jury, an end to the taxation of people earning less than thirty pounds a year, and a maximum interest rate of 6 per cent. Cromwell, in no mood to consider such reasonable proposals, rejected the Levellers' principles and suggested that "these people be cut in pieces or they will cut you in pieces." It would be fair to say that Cromwell was not someone to get on the wrong side of in an argument.

One of the more amusing results of Cromwell's actions was that many of the Levellers and sections of the New Model Army were forced to flee to the Netherlands, where their former enemy, Charlie-boy, was also in hiding. It is likely that the Levellers took a dimmer view of the pleasures to be had abroad than Charlie did, and probably spent their time complaining that they couldn't find a nice cup of tea.

Incidentally, what made the New Model Army "new" was the fact that its members received proper military training. Previously, people had become officers because they were from powerful and wealthy families. In the New Model Army, men were promoted when they showed themselves to be good soldiers. They also had a disturbing habit of going into battle singing psalms, convinced that God was on their side. So, all in all, quite a contemporary bunch.

Jack and Jill

Jack and Jill went up the hill,
To fetch a pail of water.
Jack fell down and broke his crown,
And Jill came tumbling after.

Up Jack got and home did trot,
As fast as he could caper.
He went to bed to mend his head,
With vinegar and brown paper.

Additional verse:

Then Jill came in and she did grin,
To see Jack's paper plaster.
Her mother whipped her, across her knee,
For laughing at Jack's disaster.

Let's begin with the facts that vinegar and brown paper were certainly used to draw out bruises on the body; and Jack and Jill are common names used to signify men and women (as Shakespeare said, "Jack shall have Jill and nought shall go ill"). The

197

name Jack, in particular, is used to denote any man whose name is unknown, particularly if he is a bit of a knave (thus Jack the Ripper, Spring-Heeled Jack, Jack the Lad*, etc.). Jill (Gill) also has a pleasing association with the British measure for spirits, whereas the present-day use of the term "Jacks" (from "Jack and Jills") is rhyming slang for pills. It is interesting, in view of what follows, that liquor and pills may encourage a person to dance, cause one to feel affectionate, and promote dehydration.

One saucy explanation of this rhyme is that "up the hill to fetch a pail of water" is actually a euphemism for having sex and that "losing your crown" means losing your virginity (in much the same way that people might "go to see a man about a dog" or get up to a bit of "how's your father" if they want to be vague about what they are doing). So here you have a rhyme about a young couple slipping off for a bit of "slap and tickle" and the regrets that come later. This may explain why Jill is the one most severely punished in the additional verses once her mother realizes that she has been frolicking in the hills with Jack. It is interesting that Jack runs off rapidly, probably to tell his mates about what happened.

There are claims that the rhyme can be traced to a Scandinavian folk tale explaining the markings on the surface of the moon. The story goes that the moon, or Mani, came down to Earth and captured two children, Hjuki and Bil, while they were drawing water from a well. On the night of a full moon, the pair can be seen carrying the water bucket suspended on a pole. Another notion is that the rhyme refers back to a pre-Christian tradition of gathering the first dew of May Day from a hilltop for use as a beauty treatment. Since May Day has long been associated with fertility rituals (all that phallic maypole dancing), this would appear to lead us back towards the first interpretation.

The names Jack and Jill are, as mentioned previously, ciphers for ordinary men and women and therefore tend to crop up more frequently than other names in nursery rhymes. There are at least a dozen rhymes starring Jack — "Jack Jingle" and "Jack Dandiprat" being perhaps the most amusing. The most bizarre Jack of all, though he doesn't feature in any rhyme, must be Spring-Heeled Jack, who was the first real folk devil of the industrial age. There were early sightings in poor areas of London near the Thames, where eyewitnesses reported him breathing fire and bouncing over tall buildings. There were later reports of his pranks in Liverpool and Sheffield from the mid-nineteenth century onwards. He is a unique creation, possibly a hoax perpetrated by a circus performer, and witnesses spoke of him being made of metal and rubber.

More superhero than the faith-based demons of the pre-industrial age, Spring-Heeled Jack was almost the perfect urban legend as people tried to project their fear of the modern age (machines, metal, a loss of rural habitat, etc.) onto the template of a more ancient time, the Devil. All this raises a knotty theological-cum-moral issue for environmentalists: would they rather be terrified by a traditional free-range organic demon or one of these new-fangled industrial ones?

Land of my fathers
Taffy Was a Welshman

Taffy was a Welshman, Taffy was a thief,
    Taffy came to my house
    and stole a piece of beef.
I went to Taffy's house, Taffy wasn't in,
    So I jumped upon his Sunday hat
    and poked it with a pin.

Taffy was a Welshman, Taffy was a sham,
    Taffy came to my house
    and stole a leg of lamb.
I went to Taffy's house, Taffy was away,
    So I stuffed his socks with sawdust
    and filled his shoes with clay.

Taffy was a Welshman, Taffy was a cheat,
    Taffy came to my house
    and stole a piece of meat.
I went to Taffy's house, Taffy wasn't there,
    So I hung his coat and trousers
    to roast before the fire.

As a piece of pure anti-Welsh racism, this
rhyme was used not only along the English-

Welsh borders* but also in London on St. David's Day as recently as the Second World War. It's hard to imagine now, but much of the area around King's Cross was once a Welsh ghetto. The collapse of slate-mining and other industries drove thousands to London, bringing with them an alien culture involving close-harmony singing and a fondness for cheese on toast*.

The rhyme itself supposedly goes back to the time when Welsh raiders would attack Saxon farms over the border in England, neatly disregarding the fact that those farms had once been part of Wales. So the question of who exactly is the thief in all this is quite interesting. It would not, however, be the first or last time in history that one side accused the other of crimes which they themselves had committed.

Today, English and Welsh villages straddle both sides of the "border" up to thirty miles either way, but laws allowing the execution of a Welshman after dark were only recently repealed in Chester and the Cathedral Cloister in Hereford. Border football teams such as Chester AFC, Shrewsbury, and Hereford continue a tradition of Welsh-baiting, and when they play each other chant "We hate Wrexham more than you" at opposing fans,

Wrexham being the main Welsh team close to them. They have been able to do this rather more often of late because they have all recently resided in the same semi-professional Conference League, whereas Wrexham is more successful than they and have consistently played professional football.

If a few chants and a dodgy nursery rhyme were all that the Welsh had had to suffer over the years then they could be considered to have done rather well. However, the coming of universal education was a disaster for the Welsh language. Children were dissuaded from talking in Welsh even in the playground, where something called the "Welsh Not" was passed around. This was a large block of wood with WN etched onto it, which a child had to wear when he was caught speaking Welsh, as a precursor to being punished for using too many Ls and Ys in his speech. (Welsh Scrabble, by the way, is a whole other universe.) Stories vary as to whether the children had the Welsh Not placed on them by playground prefects or whether it was passed around person to person until the end-of-break bell rang, at which point the person with the Welsh Not would have to wear it back into class and face the consequences.

Then there is the small matter of being invaded and having your conquerors build massive castles round the coastline just to reinforce the point. Though obviously Edward I, who put down the rebellion of Llewelyn ap Gruffydd, did Welsh tourism a tremendous favour by building them, it was not seen that way at the time. Edward's son, later Edward II, who was born in Caernarfon, became the first Prince of Wales.

In later years, "Prince of Wales" became the traditional title for the first-born son of a reigning monarch. Edward II skipped a generation, however, and gave the title to his grandson, Edward the Black Prince. The Black Prince's contribution to the title was the royal herald still in use today, comprising a coronet and three feathers, combined with the motto, *"Ich dien"* ("I serve," in German). This crest was the former property of blind King John of Bohemia. Before anyone gets carried away thinking it a bit unsporting that Edward stole from a blind man and maybe, for that alone, deserves the title of Black Prince, some explaining needs to be done. John of Bohemia could be considered as a prototype football hooligan who liked nothing better than to travel across Europe and join in fights that were none of his concern. His approach to battles was to have twenty knights around him who would scrap their way to where the fighting was at its densest, then leave John to hack away madly at everything around him. His unorthodox battle style was quite effective in close combat, but against archers, such as those the Black Prince employed at the battle of Crécy (1346), this approach was useless. So John lost his life and the crest, which the Black Prince took for his own, the little thief.

One everyone knows . . .

Ring-a-Ring o'Roses

Ring-a-ring o'roses,
A pocketful of Posies,
Atish-oo! Atish-oo!
We all fall down!

Of all the nursery rhymes, this is the one about which most people think they "know" the origins. One serious counter-theory to the popular one that the verses are about the Black Death is that the rhyme is actually about a children's game that allowed the young folk to get around prohibitions on dancing. This other notion is particularly strong in the United States, where extreme Puritan approaches to everyday life and actions have always been more fashionable. Regional English versions of the rhyme suggest that the falling down bit may be a curtsy, not a death rattle, as well. The relatively late appearance of this rhyme in written form also indicates that it actually came about after the worst ravages of the plague left Europe. However, the folk memory of the Black Death is very strong and a recurring motif throughout literature, even into the cinema age. So, while it is possible that the rhyme has nothing to do with dying horribly, it cannot be proved either way.

The plague (or Black Death or bubonic plague) caused devastation across Europe, particularly in the fourteenth and seventeenth centuries. In the fourteenth century, up to one-third of the population of England died, leaving villages empty, towns devastated, and cities in chaos. The last major outbreak in England was shortly before the Great Fire of London in 1666. The rebuilding of a more hygienic London after the fire is given as one cause for the plague's non-return. A nice idea, man triumphing over disease, but it was really the rats that saved the people, because the more adaptable and stronger brown rat pretty much wiped out the disease-carrying black one in Britain. The fire did clean out the old slums, but these were swiftly replaced by newer and more extensive rookeries as London's population exploded from the eighteenth century onwards.

This rhyme is thought to have been either an incantation to ward off the disease or, more likely, just a tale of the plague itself. "Ring-a-ring o'roses" describes the coloured spots that showed up on the skin. "A pocketful of posies" was an attempt to ward off illness by keeping something sweet-smelling around, a bunch (posy) of flowers. People believed that diseases were caused by evil airs (miasmas) as opposed to germs or viruses. These would, of necessity, smell bad, so could be countered by sweet-smelling things. This belief was remarkably strong. Even in the nineteenth century, cholera outbreaks in London were not linked to water but to these miasmas. It was still thought that a good smell would banish the poison. If nothing else, it would blanket the awful stench of one's fellow citizens or, during plague time, the smell of death. "Atish-oo" is the sound of sneezing, representing the physical symptoms of illness before death, when we are obliged to "all fall down."

There are apparently alternative endings that go, "Ashes, Ashes, We all fall down!" This could refer to the act of burning the deceased's clothes and personal belongings to prevent the spread of the disease, or even to the burning of bodies when they'd fallen. One problem with this version is that the burning should ordinarily come after the falling down dead. It could be referring to the funereal litany of "ashes to ashes, dust to dust." However, mass burials were more common than cremation because they were quicker, although the property of the victim was often torched.

It is time now to scotch one urban legend. There was no plague burial pit at Blackheath in south-east London. The area had its name by the twelfth century, prior to the worst plagues, and the derivation probably refers to the dark soil of this raised upland. So the popular belief that building in the area was restricted until the Second World War for fear of unleashing infection is false.

Even though the last great plague outbreak occurred in Britain in the seventeenth century, fear of the pestilence remained a part of folk memory in Europe well into the twentieth century. Indeed, the last suspected case of bubonic plague in the UK was actually in 1918, when it killed a Mrs. Garrod of Shotley, Suffolk, and possibly some of her neighbours. The disease was recognized as plague in her case only because a local man who had served in India recognized the symptoms. The terror of plague and the devastation associated with it is so etched in the collective memory that it may explain why this is the nursery rhyme that everyone "knows" the meaning of, even if it may actually just be an innocent dancing rhyme.

It's the getting there that counts

Ride a Cock Horse
to Banbury Cross

Ride a cock horse to Banbury Cross,
To see a fine lady upon a white horse.
With rings on her fingers
and bells on her toes,
She shall have music wherever she goes.

It would appear that in times past, cock horses were a popular mode of transport, and there are rhymes about a Shrewsbury Cross and a Coventry Cross. If you substitute Coventry Cross for Banbury, then perhaps this tells the story of Lady Godiva, who rode naked through Coventry as a protest against high taxes. So that's a possible explanation, but not the correct one. Nor is the notion that the lady in question is Celia Fiennes, an accomplished horsewoman from the area and part of the same annoyingly overachieving family that brought us Arctic explorers and actors in later years. It is more likely that this rhyme came into being to record the destruction of an actual ornate carved cross by some of the people of Banbury.

The county of Oxfordshire was a stronghold of Puritanism in the late sixteenth century and the folk of Banbury were famous, even within that county, for the delight they took in tearing down Papist idols such as representations of saints or — as in this case — ornate crosses. What is odd in some ways is that these English religious fanatics were keen on destroying Roman Catholic symbols but left alone the many pagan standing stones* (Great Rollrights, Little Rollrights, and so forth) in the area. Then again, without high explosives, stone can be hard to harm. It is regrettable that in recent times the Taliban found such ordnance easy to come by when they decided to destroy the ancient Buddhist monuments of Afghanistan.

The rhyme itself is a good example of British humour at work. The people of Banbury were being mocked for their zealotry, and the rhyme is clearly in the ironic tradition. For Banbury was one place where you would be most unlikely to see a fine lady on any kind of horse — far too showy, never mind all that pagan symbolism to do with white horses. Adornments such as rings and bells and, heaven forbid, music would be notable in Banbury only by their absence. This was a wind-up, in the way that apprentices were once sent off to look for left-handed spanners*. There is no double entendre in "ride a cock horse," so please remove that image from your mind right away. It just meant a feisty male horse, i.e., one that would get you there quickly, though in this instance when you did get there, there would be nothing much to see.

Britain had other famous crosses, one of which is currently in the Metropolitan Museum of Art, in New York City. Known in Britain as the Bury Cross, after Bury St. Edmunds, the Suffolk town where it is believed to have been made, the Bury Cross is one of the greatest works of medieval art in the world. Made in the twelfth century, it is exquisitely carved from walrus tusk but has a very dark history. It was essentially a rallying point for anti-Semitism, a sort of medieval swastika, used to incite the massacre of Bury St. Edmunds's Jews in 1190. The cross has a litany of anti-Jewish inscriptions carved minutely along its twenty-inch length. Perhaps unfortunately, it missed the attentions of the Puritans because it was travelling around

213

Europe at the time. Having once formed part of the bounty paid for the ransomed King Richard the Lionheart, it spent most of its life in Norway before finding its way to New York.

It might be better to end on a cheerier note and return to Lady Godiva. She is immortalized in cockney rhyming slang in the term "lady" to mean "five pounds," the reason being that "Lady Godiva" rhymes with "fiver." So that's all quite nice and logical. The term for "fifteen pounds" is "commodore," however, under the slightly more convoluted rationale that fifteen is three times five (a lady) and "Three Times a Lady" was a big hit for the band the Commodores. Simple when you get the hang of it.

Kitty Fisher, now she's a sort*

Lucy Locket

Lucy Locket lost her pocket
Kitty Fisher found it
Not a penny was there in it
But a ribbon round it.

As with the "Grand Old Duke of York," there are a couple of candidates for the role of Kitty Fisher. Some sources believe that Kitty and Lucy were rival courtesans at the court of Charles II. According to this version, Kitty Fisher picks up Lucy's beau but finds him broke. While this might be an interesting take on the meaning of the rhyme, it is not the true origin.

There was a real Kitty Fisher, with pictures to prove it that hang in the National Portrait Gallery in London and at Petworth House, East Sussex. She lived at Hemsted House in Kent with her husband, John Norris, during the reign of George II. However, Kitty wasn't "to the manor born";* she had to earn her passage there. The daughter of a milliner, she worked her way up through society via various bedchambers. She had the example of Nell Gwynn (who rose from orange seller to the King's mistress) and many others to follow. Kitty has been denigrated by some historians as something of a gold digger with questionable morals but her description on the National Portrait Gallery Web site reads:

Catherine Maria ("Kitty") Fisher (died 1767), Courtesan. Known for her beauty, wit and daring horsemanship.

There is no questioning her beauty, and if you want to see for yourself you could check out one of the above-mentioned portraits. Her fame reached its height in the 1750s (when a portrait of her was commissioned), more than fifty years after the heyday of the court of Charles II.

In her early years she worked at a high-class brothel in Covent Garden favoured by George II (1727–1760). One story about her time there is fantastic and concerns that well-known librarian Casanova (it's true, look it up). Apparently, Casanova offered Kitty ten pounds (a great deal of money at the time) to go to bed with him but she refused because, to paraphrase Naomi Campbell, she wouldn't get into bed for less than fifteen.

When she settled into the role of mistress of Hemsted, she was popular with the local folk because she was generous to the poor and very upbeat at all times. Unfortunately, she died of smallpox soon after moving to the country. Her last wish was to be buried in the churchyard dressed in her best ballgown, which must have been a challenge for the funeral directors. Overall Kitty was admired as a beautiful and ambitious woman with a generous spirit who did very well for herself. Hemsted House is now home to one of England's premier girl's boarding schools. Established in 1923, it aims to be a "happy school with personal integrity and service to others in mind, where everyone shall be given the chance to follow her own bent." Seems like a fitting epitaph for the lovely Kitty.

So Kitty was a popular girl with plenty of zest, just the sort of inspirational figure people would want to sing songs about. There was once a great tradition of popular song and verse about heroes of the age, which now only really survives in Britain to any large extent around football. Today, of course, popular heroes are saluted in other ways, perhaps given a newspaper column, or a respectful (or, better yet, disrespectful) documentary is aired about them.

This is all very well and good but the rhyme makes sense only if we know who Lucy Locket was. The name is used in *The Beggar's Opera* to denote "everywoman" and this might be the answer. Kitty found her prize (true love and nice house in the country) but in doing so denied that prize (at least that particular eligible bachelor) to others. Sadly, this was a slightly hollow success because she died soon after. So the rhyme is a roundabout way of saying "beware of what you wish for."

For no reason other than it's a nice tale and shows that some mistresses do very well indeed, it is worth mentioning Nell Gwynn again. She was bequeathed a house on Pall Mall by Charles II. To this day it is the only independent freehold* property on Pall Mall; all the other freeholds are held by the Crown Estate. When Charles's lawyers offered her the leasehold, she declared that she had always lain freely with the King and held him freely and would expect nothing less than the freehold on the property. So, good for her.

Pop Goes the Weasel

Half a pound of tuppenny rice,
Half a pound of treacle.
That's the way the money goes,
Pop! goes the weasel.

Johnny's got the whooping cough,
And Mary's got the measles.
That's the way the money goes,
Pop! goes the weasel.

Up and down the City Road,
In and out the Eagle.
That's the way the money goes,
Pop! goes the weasel.

A penny for a ball of thread,
Another for a needle,
That's the way the money goes,
Pop! goes the weasel.

All around the cobbler's bench
The monkey chased the people.
The donkey thought 'twas all in fun,
Pop! goes the weasel.

One other variant goes:

All around the mulberry bush
The monkey chased the weasel.
The monkey thought 'twas all in fun.
Pop! goes the weasel.

There are many, many extra verses to this one, and the most common British version of the rhyme seems to be a fairly literal, early Victorian (1850s) song that bled from the music halls to the streets to become a skit on how the poor spent their money. It is possibly based on an earlier rhyme about silk weavers but, in its current form, only the optional mulberry bush and possibly the "weasel" popping have any connection with the earlier song.

The silk weavers themselves were French Protestants (Huguenots) who settled in London in the seventeenth century. They fled France after the Edict of Nantes (a statute guaranteeing religious freedom) was revoked in 1685. They settled in Soho and Spitalfields in London and also in Brandenburg in Germany. Those who settled in Spitalfields, in east London, were highly skilled silk weavers. Interestingly, they set the pattern for the area for the next three hundred years. The next big wave of refugees, Jews from Eastern Europe, also settled in Spitalfields and also took up the rag trade, as did the Bangladeshis in the late twentieth century. (The word "refugee" came to the English language with the Huguenots.) They established themselves in the area, before, like subsequent waves of migrants, moving on.

As well as being a traditional immigrant reception area, Spitalfields and nearby Hoxton were the centre of music hall, a rough theatre with sketches, songs, short plays, and comedy. It was hugely popular, making up a third of all theatre seats in London before the genre's demise with the coming of cinema, and later television, in the twentieth century.

In the rhyme, the "weasel" popping is thought to refer to the sound of the spinning machine at the end of its cycle and the "mulberry bush" is what silkworms feed on (see "Here We Go Round the Mulberry Bush"). This is not the only connection with the schmutter* trade in the East End. "Weasel" is also rhyming slang for coat ("weasel and stoat") and to "pop" something means to pawn it. Other authorities believe that the "weasel" was a short flat iron used by tailors in the course of their trade, while in the criminal slang of the 1850s "weasel" meant something silver, especially watches. So a fair range of items that could be popped, but the essential point is the same: a series of expenditures, followed by the pawning of something to defray those costs. The suggestion that parts of the rhyme are early Victorian is substantiated by the written records of some of the music-hall acts.

Of course, this does raise the question of what the monkey is doing there. In East End slang, the term "monkey" means five hundred pounds, and "monkey's tails" is rhyming slang for "nails," as is "monkey wrench" for "bench." Both might fit well into a rhyme based around a workshop. That's very hard to prove, however, as hammering down the origin of a particular rhyming-slang phrase can be tricky.

One even dodgier theory is that the "monkey" is a Frenchman. This is based on the prejudiced view that the English had (have?) of the French. This view was so extreme that, according to legend, when a monkey survived a shipwreck off the north-east coast near Hartlepool during the Napoleonic wars (1799–1815), it was hanged as a suspected French spy. The monkey did not help its defence by being dressed in a French navy uniform when it was found, or by refusing to answer its interrogators (some local fishermen) in English. The sounds that came from the monkey were assumed to be French, and so the monkey was strung up at the beach.

An Eagle pub still stands at the original site on the corner of Shepherdess Walk and the City Road in Islington. At one time the Eagle contained a theatre — the Old Grecian Saloon and Olympic Temple — built by a Mr. Thomas Rouse and later taken over by Mr. Benjamin Conquest in 1851. The latter gentleman is celebrated in a lesser-known version of the rhyme that honoured London theatres and their owners. The lines about the Eagle in this version go:

In the bird of Conquest, made
First by Romans Famous.
Though Grecian my saloon was called,
By some ignoramus.

Up and down the City Road
In and out the Eagle etc. . . .

The odd couple

Jack Spratt

Jack Spratt could eat no fat,
His wife could eat no lean.
And so betwixt them both,
They licked the platter clean.

Interpreted directly, this is a celebration of
that rarest of things: a happily married
couple who complement each other perfectly. The first recorded version is:

Jack will eat no fat and Jill doth love
   no lean,
Yet betwixt them both they lick the
   dishes clean.

Of course, this notion of a cheerful bal-
ance in a relationship between adults
would be far too implausible for the
modern child to accept, so it is perhaps
better to go with the theory that this rhyme
is about Charles I and could well have
started life as a call to arms by the
Roundheads. Certainly, the fact that the

early version can be dated as far back as 1639 would add to the authenticity of this story.

The explanation goes that Charles I of England and his wife, Henrietta Maria, were refused finance by Parliament for a proposed war with Spain. This left Charles a bit overdrawn, meaning he could eat no fat because there wasn't any. His wife's extravagant tastes meant she couldn't abide lean, or poor, times. So he dissolved Parliament, then, along with his wife, imposed a war tax, forced common people to house the troops, and imposed other taxes to pay for his wife's luxuries. So this original odd couple licked England clean one way or another.

The term "Jack Spratt" was also used in the sixteenth and seventeenth centuries to mean "person of restricted growth," in addition to the even more delightful "Jack Dandiprat" to denote an "irksome small boy." There is a fascination with little people as figures of fun, metaphor, and fear throughout British history, but the person who took this fascination to its logical extreme was Queen Anne. One of our more eccentric monarchs, she was ruling when the Act of Union with Scotland was signed in 1707 and Gibraltar was finally established as British. She has been portrayed as a tea-drinking social inadequate with lesbian tendencies, who grew so stout that she had to be buried in a square coffin. This barely scratches the surface, though. For example, how many other monarchs have a range of furniture and a soup (Queen Anne broth) named after them? Or how many kept a retinue of very small people in attendance for state occasions alongside, just for maximum contrast, the tallest man in the kingdom? None, is the answer.

Back to the rhyme: it seems a shame that Charles and Henrietta were punished for their eating habits, and Charles, of course, lost his head after the Civil War. A shame, because it is rare that a married royal couple are in such perfect accord, and in this regard they could certainly embarrass some of their descendants.

Wages of sin?

See Saw, Marjorie Daw

See saw, Marjorie Daw,
Johnny shall have a new master,
Jacky shall have but a penny a day,
Because he can't work any faster.

This is apparently an old sawing song, used
to keep a steady rhythm and ensure a
straighter cut. More recently, the rhyme became something children sang on a see-saw
as they played. It is tempting to imagine
Marjorie as some kind of Gradgrind*,
blocking Johnny's path to promotion and
asserting that shop-floor toilers should be
thankful for their pitiful wages. And it
would be perfectly natural to find an English rhyme hymning the Protestant work
ethic, unless we consider the other version
of the rhyme, which goes like this:

See saw, Majory Daw,
Sold her bed and lay on straw,
Sold her bed and lay on hay,
Till Pisky came and took her away,

227

For wasn't she the dirty slut,
To sell her bed and lay in muck?

That's much more like it! "Majory" was a common country name and "pisky" is Cornish for "fairy." Even better, "daw" means "slattern," or "lazy, slovenly person." So perhaps this is a slur on country folk for living like pigs or just a general warning that if you don't keep your room tidy, the fairies will come for you and they're not going to leave money for your teeth. They are going to take your teeth, and you with them.

Fairies, spirits, and the like, perhaps surprisingly, get very few mentions in nursery rhymes and they are not friendly in this one. The idea of Pisky taking away the trollop, Ms. Daw, is almost akin to the idea of the Devil coming for the soul of evildoers. This belief was very strong across Britain and, in one event, hundreds of people swore that they saw Old Nick coming for the soul of a witch, Mother Damnable, who lived in a cottage near Camden Town tube. This is quite possibly the first, some might say only, interesting thing that has happened in this part of north London, an area that today acts as a magnet for people wearing black clothes, adorned with strange icons, and with a fondness for the occult. Ironically, this is exactly the sort of behaviour that got Ms. Damnable into trouble in the first place.

It seems that the phrase "away with the fairies" could mean something darker than its traditional meaning of being "absent-minded." According to legend, fairies were not averse to switching their own children with those of humans when they found their own offspring ugly. The result gave rise to the phenomenon of the "changeling," the runt fairy-child raised by humans who wreaks evil on his or her adoptive household. Naturally, a more logical explanation is that the human family used this as an excuse for the child's shortcomings or failure to look like its parents. In a time before genetics was understood, a child who was a throwback to an earlier generation might indeed appear strange. This ties in rather nicely with another theory about the strength of belief in fairies and other beings in Britain. This holds that fairies were the original Britons, driven to the margins of forests and swamps, away from the conquering Celts, Romans, Saxons, etc., etc.

Getting back to Pisky, there seems to be quite a range of these bad fairies: banshees to foretell death with their keening wail and leprechauns to trick you, as well as pixies to play pranks and lead the simple-minded astray. Perhaps it's better to end on a more upbeat note, with some good fairies. Gnomes and elves can be friendly to humans, and there are tales of them helping travellers lost in the wilds. Oddly, these favours were returned in Iceland recently, where belief in the *huldfolk,* or "land wights," is so strong that they are consulted on major construction projects. Apparently the orbital motorway around Iceland is the shape it is because it was diverted to avoid burrows and boulders sacred to the little folk.

Old King Cole
Was a Merry Old Soul

Old King Cole was a merry old soul,
And a merry old soul was he.
He called for his pipe,
and he called for his bowl,
And he called for his fiddlers three.

Every fiddler he had a fiddle,
And a very fine fiddle had he.
Oh there's none so rare,
As can compare,
With King Cole and his fiddlers three.

Oh, but there's all manner of fun to be had
with this rhyme, which is traceable back to
the Middle Ages and purports to be about
the antics of a cheery British king called
Cole. To the modern reader, it's clear that
the King might have every reason to be a
bit lit, what with people bringing him pipes
and bowls. A more traditional reading is
that the pipe referred to would almost cer-

tainly be some kind of wind instrument and the bowl is in all probability an instrument similar to the Irish bodhran drum. So, with the pipe and bowl, what we have is the fact that the old King liked his music, not that the King liked his narcotics, even if cannabis use was traced to at least as far back as A.D. 400 and a later monarch, Queen Victoria, was given hash by her doctor to relieve period pains.

Now, the question is, did King Cole exist as a real person or does he embody the yearning of the British people for a lost golden age? Or a future one of pipe and slippers? Geoffrey of Monmouth, who wrote a history of Britain in the twelfth century, appears to think that a King Cole ruled part of the country, though which part and when are other issues altogether. According to one legend, Old King Cole is said to have built Colchester, whereas in another variant "Coel Hen," to give him his original name, is thought to have ruled south-west Scotland, Cumbria, and bits of Yorkshire. Some believe he was related to Welsh nobility, which seems plausible, as "hen" is Welsh for "old" or "aged." It is worth remembering that Welsh in this context refers not to what we think of as Wales but to the older inhabitants of these isles, the Britons in general. For example, the name Walworth, given to an area near the Elephant and Castle in south London, means "farm of the Britons," despite there being no agricultural activity and precious few Welsh people in the area's rich multi-cultural mix.

The connection with Colchester is charming but unlikely, as the city was already inhabited by the seventh century B.C. and was known as Camulodunum ("Fortress of the war god Camulos") by the early A.D. period. The Saxons referred to it as Colneceaste, suggesting that the current name comes from the River Colne, which runs through the city, and "chester" comes from *castra,* the Roman word for "armed camp." The old tribal capital was an early target of the Roman invaders (A.D. 43) and within a few years they had converted it into Roman Britain's first colony of retired legionaries and the administrative centre of the area. The most famous King Cole who appears on the scene later is nowt to do with East Anglia. Coel Hen was a northern warlord ruling an area from southern Scotland to Merseyside who fought against the Picts and Scots until his death in 420. King Henry VIII claimed descent from Coel's dynasty, and legend has it that he was the grandfather of the magician Merlin.

Some regard Coel Hen as Britain's first Dark Age king. His ancestry connects him to Britain's pre-Roman nobility and his descendants became lords and princes of huge areas of northern England, southern Scotland, and north-east Wales. However, whether he was truly a king or just a Roman tribal ally in place to keep the Scots busy is a debating point. He was fond of fiddling, in common with a certain Mr. Nero, and seems to have been well regarded enough historically for the nursery rhyme to be composed in his honour, albeit centuries later.

Many more centuries on there was another King Cole, who has nothing whatsoever to do with the original rhyme but whose tale is well worth telling. A small plaque on a eucalyptus tree in a park in Bethnal Green, east London, simply says, "1868 King Cole Aborigine Cricketer." It serves as a memorial to one member of a team of Aborigine cricketers who toured England. Interestingly, this was nine years before any official (for which read "white") Australian side ever came over to beat the English at their own game, complain about the weather, and work in pubs in west

London. The Strine* authorities were less than happy about a bunch of dark fellows representing "their" territory, but the British were fine about it, except that they had problems with the team members' names. To anyone familiar with football commentary over the past few decades, this should come as no great surprise and rather than have a nineteenth-century Mr. Coleman* balls up the Aborigines' names, it was decided to rename the whole team. The star player was dubbed "Dick a Dick," another was renamed "Sundown," and Bripumyarrimin came to be called "King Cole." The team did well in cricketing terms, coming close to beating the MCC* at Lord's*. However, they were bowled over by a range of diseases, and King Cole sadly died at a Bethnal Green hospital after a spell with pneumonia. In a very touching gesture, local people planted an Australian tree in his honour, and that's where his plaque remains. It has subsequently become a site of pilgrimage for visiting teams of Aborigine cricketers. While the cricketing "King Cole" had clearly touched local people and may have been a jolly fellow, there is no record of whether he was fond of music.

We British like our mythical kings, and

Cole with his rhyme is right up there with Arthur and his round table and Lud with his hill in London. Arthur, and to a lesser extent Cole, began to be popular figures in the Middle Ages, as whenever crisis struck, people could fondly say, "Well, of course, if we had King Arthur back, we wouldn't have any bother with those Normans and the rest of that European crowd." Much in the way that today men of a certain age (and disposition) go alarmingly misty-eyed when the words "Europe" and "Margaret Thatcher" are mentioned in the same sentence. King Lud was not resurrected until much later, when he was evoked under the guise of Ned Lud, whose machine-wrecking antics in the early Industrial Revolution brought the word Luddite into the English language to describe a person who opposes new technology and looks back to a (supposedly) golden past. The legendary King Cole was fond of a tune, and the likely explanation for the rhyme is that it is a song celebrating a lost golden age with a happy king and a country at peace and full of music. There is a strange human tendency to look back to the past for a happier, more innocent time (sociologists are very precise about this, explaining that the golden age is *always* exactly fifty years earlier), which, if you wanted to get psychoanalytical about it, could be put down to a yearning for the lost joys and certainties of childhood. Unless it's something we pick up in childhood through cheery rhymes . . .

A Brief Note
About Sources

Heavy Words was never meant to be a particularly scholarly exercise, so apologies if you were expecting a lengthy bibliography. As some of you are no doubt aware, there are many alternative theories for several of the rhymes featured here, but this book has gone for the most interesting and plausible in its search for the reason behind the rhyme. Research has been drawn from a wide range of sources, encompassing television, film, radio, books, newspapers and magazines, oral tradition, theatre, hearsay, the Internet, and straightforward gossip. Should you wish to delve deeper into the subject, three books that proved very useful were:

Opie, Iona and Peter, eds., *The Oxford Dictionary of Nursery Rhymes.* Oxford University Press, 1992 edition
Rollin, Lucy, *Cradle and All: A Cultural and Psychoanalytic Reading of Nursery*

Rhymes. University of Mississippi
Press, 1992
Warner, Marina, *No Go the Bogeyman:
Scaring, Lulling and Making Mock.*
Farrar, Straus and Giroux, 1998

The following books were good for background material:

Ackroyd, Peter, *London the Biography.*
Chatto and Windus, 2000
Cowie, Leonard W., *Plague and Fire:
London 1665–66.* Wayland, 1970
Mayhew, Henry, *London Labour and the
London Poor.* Dover Publications, 1968
Pearson, Geoffrey, *Hooligan: A History of
Respectable Fears.* Macmillan Press,
1983

Glossary

13. Boffin: Originally, armed forces slang for research scientist or technician. Overused by British tabloids to signify (and often subtly undermine) an expert in any field. US equivalents are "Egghead," and, perhaps among the younger generation, "Poindexter."

14. Squatted: Unofficially occupied vacated premises, usually residential.

18. Football: Soccer, as it is quaintly known in the US, is by and large referred to as football in the rest of the world. While the term soccer is understood throughout the planet, most genuine fans avoid its use in the manner that the term gridiron is rarely used in the United States. See also pp. 20, 23, 73, 76, 122, 203, 204, 217, 235.

18. Football chants: Football chants and songs are sung loudly every week at matches. They can be historic, dating back to the formation of the club, adaptations of popular songs, or spontaneous reactions to events on the pitch. They are one of the last remaining sources of an oral folk song tradition in the UK in that they are generally copyright free, noncommercial, and directly reflect people's hopes and emotions. See also pp. 73, 76, 122, 203, 217.

18. Rhyming slang: A form of slang in which a word is replaced by a rhyming word or phrase. Confusingly, the actual rhyming part is usually omitted, e.g. "Sherman" for US citizen (Sherman tank = Yank). See also pp. 81, 198, 214, 221, 222.

20. Koppites: Collective term for supporters of Liverpool Football Club. The home supporters' end at Anfield is named The Kop, after Spion Kop, scene of a major battle in the Boer War. Kop is Dutch for "look-out hill" and a common name for a mountain in South Africa.

22. Act of Union: The legislative incorporation of England and Scotland in 1707. See also pp. 100, 225.

23. Goodison Park: Stadium in Liverpool, home of Everton Football Club.

23. Scouser: A person who comes from Liverpool. See p. 162.

23. Giro: Government cheque paid to the unemployed. In the 1980s Liverpool suffered very high levels of unemployment.

28. Ye Olde Currant Bun: "Currant bun" is rhyming slang for *The Sun*, a well-known tabloid newspaper keen on salacious stories.

29. Ken Russell: British filmmaker overly obsessed with sexuality and the church.

43. Razzle: To be "out on the razzle" means to go out and get drunk; "appearing in it" alludes to the British adult (we say "top shelf") magazine of the same name that specialises in naked pictures of readers' wives.

47. Dub: Originally a style of poetry of West Indian origin, performed spontaneously to a reggae beat. Dub music, developed in Jamaica in the early 1970s, characteristically involves revisions of existing songs. Totally unrelated is the fact that "rub-a-dub" is rhyming slang for pub.

52. SE1: London's post (zip) codes are

confusing even to most Londoners. In the mid-nineteenth century, central London postal districts were split between east and west central (EC and WC, broadly the City and the West End), while the outer parts of inner London were split into N, NW, NE, S, SW, SE, W, and E. NE and S were later dropped and are now used for Newcastle and Sheffield, respectively. When the modern postcode system was introduced in the 1960s, numerals were added, with the nearest areas in each direction allocated the number one (N1, SE1, etc.). Thereafter, numbers were allocated alphabetically, rather than geographically, and with complete disregard to the boundaries of London's boroughs. So a southeasterly journey on the major roads out of SE1 (South Bank/Waterloo/Borough) takes you in sequence through SE17 (Walworth), SE5 (Camberwell), SE14 (New Cross), SE13 (Lewisham), SE12 (Lee), then SE9 (Eltham).

52. Tube: Common slang for the London Underground network, its trains and stations (on account of the circular tunnels). See also pp. 169, 228.

55. Parliamentarian: Supporters of Cromwell during the English Civil War against

King Charles I, also known as Roundheads. Royalists (the king's supporters) were alternatively known as Cavaliers.

59. Grassing up: Informing on.

62. Nice young girls who used to appear in the comic *Bunty*: Marys Radleigh, Simpson, Cotter, and Field were characters in this long-running comic strip for girls.

64. Charlie Dimmock: One of the hosts on the BBC gardening makeover show, *Ground Force.* Water features are her speciality (along with going braless under a T-shirt in all weather).

67. Lollards: Followers of John Wycliffe; lay preachers in fourteenth- and fifteenth-century England and Scotland.

68. Eddie Izzard: Top British comedian and actor, also known for his transvestitism.

79. Copping off: Generic term for mild sexual activity also used to describe an agreement to a first date. If you "copped off" with someone, you probably only got to first base. The related term "getting off with" definitely means full sex.

85. Spot-on: Exactly right or just so.

88. Schemey tea: In Scotland, council estates (public housing) are known as schemes. The phrase "schemey tea" is therefore a derogatory way of saying "poor person's supper."

88. Council blocks: Public housing projects.

95. On the never-never: Paying for something by hire purchase.

97. Four-eyed: As well as being a derogatory term for "bespectacled," "four eyes" is prison slang for a child sex offender. The Rev. Dodgson's fondness for the original Alice is commonly alleged to have had a sexual basis.

98. Blur and Oasis: The simultaneous release of albums and singles sparked a media-fuelled "battle of the bands" between southern upper-middle-class school chums Blur and northern working-class Beatles wannabes Oasis. Damon Albarn and Noel Gallagher are the creative forces behind the respective bands (only don't say as much in front of Liam Gallagher).

102. Trannie: Transvestite. Not to be confused with Trinny, who is one half of the BBC's *What Not to Wear* team.

103. Biscuits: Cookies, which I personally think is the better word, as a character called Biscuit Monster would never have worked.

103. Alexei Sayle: Marxist stand-up comedian, writer, and actor (and there's not many of those about).

104. *Blackadder*: Historical BBC comedy series starring Rowan Atkinson.

108. Outward Bound: Any extracurricular activity that takes place away from the school — from hill walking to canoeing.

108. League tables: Ranking of schools by government inspectors to rigid guidelines that fail to take into account broader social conditions, with the result that failing schools are often made worse as more ambitious parents avoid them.

109. The God Ford: Reference to the theory of post-Fordism (i.e., post-industrial capitalism).

110. A few stops beyond Barking: Barking is an area of east London, and a station on the London Underground. To be "barking" is short for "barking mad," i.e., crazy. To be "a few stops beyond Barking" (or "totally Dagenham," which is a few stops after Barking on the District Line) means to be completely insane.

110. Barmy: Crazy, foolish. See also p. 114.

114. M25; M25 corridor: London orbital motorway designed to divert cars and trucks from central London, but renowned for its traffic congestion; the area around it.

115. Barnsley: Small town in Yorkshire, a couple of hundred miles north of London geographically, but several time zones away culturally, according to some cruel observers.

117. Guineas: Obsolete coins (1663–1813) equalling one pound and one shilling, originally made of gold brought from Guinea in Africa. Still favoured as a unit of currency among the horse-racing fraternity and certain professions.

122. Fivers: Five-pound notes.

125. Clive of India: Worked for the East India Company before transferring to the military. Achieved a famous victory by holding off ten thousand enemy troops armed with sharp bits of stick with just two hundred soldiers armed with automatic rifles. Subsequently became an MP and made a good deal of money before returning to Bengal to restore good government. He is credited with securing India (and the wealth that followed) for the British crown.

128. Dial 999: The equivalent of dialling 911 in emergencies.

128. James Howell: Seventeenth-century historian and writer.

129. Inns of Court: Inner Temple, Middle Temple, Lincoln's Inn, and Gray's Inn in Central London. All barristers serving in English courts must belong to one of these institutions.

129. John Evelyn: Contemporary and friend of Samuel Pepys whose most famous work, his *Diary* or *Memoirs*, has been eclipsed over time by Pepys's own chronicles of seventeenth-century life.

132. Foster: Facetiously applied collective noun, after Sir Norman Foster, Britain's most prolific builder of landmark office developments.

138. Mothercare: Chain of stores specializing in baby clothes, toys, and maternity wear. In 2003 (a month before the first edition of this book came out in the UK), Mothercare released a CD of nursery rhymes which made all the endings happy so that, for example, Humpty Dumpty was put back together again.

143. Thatcher, turning: The key reference is to a speech Mrs. Thatcher made at the Conservative Party conference in 1980. At the time her policies were causing mass unemployment and civil unrest across Britain and there was a great deal of talk in the media about the need for a policy U-turn. Referring to this speculation in the speech she said, "You turn if you want to. The lady's not for turning." That same evening she was seen on a dance floor executing some very fine turns at the end-of-conference ball.

146. Millwall FC: Millwall Football Club, despite their best efforts of late, have an enduring reputation for having some of the rowdiest supporters in English football. For decades home fixtures rarely passed without some sort of disturbance, and the area around their ground in Bermondsey on the final weekend of the season still echoes to the sounds of brawling and police sirens.

146. Costermongers: Originally sellers of fruit (in particular the coster apple) but now used to describe street traders in general.

146. Mobiles: Cell phones.

147. Panto: Short for pantomime, a traditional Christmas entertainment used to save the careers of fading entertainers.

157. EC1: See SE1 (p. 242)

158. Gaol: Alternative spelling of "jail."

162. Scallies: "Scallie" or "scally" is short for scallywag originally but in the Liverpool (and Manchester) context refers more to fashion-conscious hooligans.

163. Lobskaus: Also "lobscouse": Stew or hash, usually fish based.

165. Parkin: Also "perkin": A soft cake made of oatmeal and molasses.

168. IRA: Irish Republican Army. Armed Irish Nationalist movement. Interestingly quiet of late after the Good Friday Agreement to share power in Northern Ireland and the fine work of former Maine Senator George Mitchell. However, those of a more cynical frame of mind cite the withdrawal of Irish expatriate funding after 9/11 as a bigger reason for the IRA's cessation of violence.

169. Bollards: Short posts arranged in a line to prevent the passage of motor vehicles.

169. CCTV: Closed-Circuit Television Cameras are proving very useful to low-budget TV producers throughout the UK for programmes along the lines of *World's Rudest Drunks Outside Nightclubs in the North of England.* More worryingly they follow the British public as they go about their daily chores in the nation's shopping malls and other unrestricted spaces.

170. British Summer Time: The equivalent of Daylight Saving Time, where the clocks are put forward to fool farmers into believing they have an extra hour in bed.

170. Samhain: The end of the Celtic year (and the origin of Halloween).

170. Beltane: Last of three spring fertility festivals, heralding the beginning of summer.

177. Battersea Council: Local government assembly in southwest London. Interestingly Battersea had not only Britain's first black mayor but also one of only two communist members of Parliament. Even better, in view of the story, is the fact that the UK's most famous refuge for stray dogs is in Battersea.

187. Taking the piss: To mock, tease, or scoff (deride).

198. Jack the Lad: Flashy, cocksure young man (*see also* Scallie, p. 250).

201. English–Welsh Borders: It's a linguistic curiosity that in the UK the internal boundary regions between England and Wales (and England and Scotland) are referred to as "the Borders" rather than "the border." Perhaps this is due to the fact that although we are one nation, we are several nationalities, and it makes sense to us that looking at the same thing from two sides means there are two borders, not one. For the Welsh, a Welsh–English border and for the English, an English–Welsh border.

202. Close-harmony singing and a fondness for cheese on toast: Arbitrary racist stereotypes for which the author offers the defence that he is himself part Welsh and can therefore get away with it. The latter part refers to Welsh rarebit (or rabbit), which is melted cheese on hot toast at its best when the cheese is first mixed with a drop of ale.

212. Standing stones: Great stones erect in the ground, usually set in a circular, oval, or horseshoe-shaped construction, or "henge." Sites of ancient religious ceremonies, sometimes containing burial chambers.

213. Spanners: Wrenches.

215. Now she's a sort: is Southeast London slang for "babe." Can also be applied to an attractive male.

215. "To the manor born": *To the Manor Born* was a BBC sitcom about a woman of high birth fallen on hard times, who had to sell the family home to a nouveau riche entrepreneur (and went on to marry him to regain her birthright). It is a play on the phrase "to the manner born," which means to be accomplished at a certain trade or skill.

218. Freehold: In English law a freehold means a person owns the land on which a building stands as well as the building, whereas with a leasehold (which may be for as long as 999 years), the property reverts back to the owner of the land after the lease period has elapsed. A good example is the US embassy in the UK, which stands on land leased from the Duke of Westminster and is the only US embassy in the world where the US government does not own the land the embassy stands on. The Duke in question refused to grant the freehold because after the US War of Independence Washington's boys stole — as he saw it — some of his ancestors' estates in Virginia.

219. Adam and Eve: Rhyming slang for "believe."

221. Schmutter: Yiddish slang for "clothing" or "rag."

227. Gradgrind: Thomas Gradgrind, character in Charles Dickens's *Hard Times* dedicated to the pursuit of profitable enterprise.

235. Strine: Mildly dismissive term for "Australian" based on the antipodean habit of reducing polysyllabic words into a single sound.

235. Mr. Coleman: David Coleman, British sports broadcaster so adept at getting names wrong, spouting clichés, and generally making asinine comments that the satirical magazine *Private Eye* created a column in his honour, called "Colemanballs," that collects the stupid utterances of commentators and other public figures.

235. MCC: Marylebone Cricket Club, the world's oldest and most famous cricket club, which was founded in 1787, and laid down the laws of the game a year later.

235. Lord's: The MCC's cricket ground in St. John's Wood, north-west London. The self-styled "home of cricket" is named for Thomas Lord, bowler and entrepreneur.